lights shining in the darkness

men of faith

PETER JEFFREY

lights shining
in the darkness

men of faith

EVANGELICAL PRESS

EVANGELICAL PRESS
Faverdale North Industrial Estate, Darlington, DL3 0PH, England

Evangelical Press USA
P. O. Box 84, Auburn, MA 01501, USA

e-mail: sales@evangelicalpress.org

web: www.evangelicalpress.org

First published 2003

British Library Cataloguing in Publication Data available

ISBN 0 85234 505 4

Printed and bound in Great Britain by Creative Print & Design Wales, Ebbw Vale

Contents

	page
Augustine & Athanasius	8
John Wycliffe	16
Martin Luther	26
William Tyndale	36
Oliver Cromwell	44
Daniel Rowland	60
Jonathan Edwards	70
Whitefield in America	84
Nettleton & Finney	96
Finally	109

Introduction

Church history is a field rich in spiritual blessings. It tells us of God's dealings with men and women down through the centuries. Some of the stories are reminiscent of the Acts of the Apostles – amazing incidents that can only be explained by a supernatural intervention of God. Other stories are more what we would call normal, but supernatural or normal, all relate to the activity of God in and through his people. No Christian can fail to benefit from knowing of these things, but the sad truth is that few believers walk in this field.

Most Christians know of the great names of church history through mention of them in sermons, but that is about as far as it goes. This book is written to introduce you to some of the great men of the past. The choice of men to consider is enormous and the ones included are simply men I have always been interested in. They are those who had a passionate love for the Lord and his word and were willing to take on the world in the name of Christ.

It is impossible in a book of this size to do justice to such spiritual giants and therefore it is hoped that you will go on and read more for yourself.

Athanasius of Alexandria (296-373)

Augustine of Hippo (354-430)

Chapter 1

Athanasius and Augustine

The fourth and fifth centuries saw great battles in the church over doctrine and several heresies that still plague the church today were born during this period. Up to this point the church had been fighting for survival as one persecution after another attacked it. A change occurred in 312 A.D. when Constantine (280-337), a sun-worshipper and Emperor of Britain, France and Spain, defeated in battle the larger army of the anti-Christian Emperor Maxentius, who ruled over Italy and North-West Africa. Constantine believed that his victory had come from God and from then on professed faith in Christianity. Suddenly it became fashionable to be a Christian. Thousands, who had no experience of a living faith in Christ, joined the church and days of persecution were replaced with days of spiritual and theological slackness. This was an ideal climate in which heresy could flourish.

Athanasius of Alexandria (296-373) and Augustine of Hippo (354-430), were the prominent defenders of the biblical faith in this period.

Athanasius of Alexandria

An elder of the Alexandrian church named Arius (256-336), taught that although Christ was closer to God than any other being, he had still been created and therefore was not fully God in the same sense as God the Father. Arius was opposed by Bishop Alexander and a bitter controversy which affected the whole church, developed between these two men. The Emperor Constantine, who had no understanding of doctrine but did not want the church to be divided, advised Alexander and Arius not to dispute over trifles. But the deity of Christ is the heart of the Christian faith, not a trifle of little consequence.

The controversy did not go away and in 325 AD Constantine brought together bishops from all over the Empire and formed 'The Council of Nicaea'. It was the first of two councils set up to try and settle the Arian controversy. The bishops produced the Creed of Nicaea which states that Christ is the Son of God in every respect and that Christ was ' begotten of the Father ... begotten, not created, of the same essence as the Father.' It affirmed the unity of God and stated that '[we believe] in the Holy Spirit'.[1]

Arius refused to sign the creed and with three other bishops was sent into exile by Constantine. Unity seemed to be restored to the church but it was only a veneer and concealed underlying deep divisions. Three years after the Council of Nicaea Alexander died and Athanasius became the new Bishop of Alexandria. By this time Constantine wanted Arius restored to the church but Athanasius, realising the seriousness of Arius's heresy, refused point blank. He saw that Arianism was totally against the heart of the Christian gospel for it reduced Christ to the level of a demi-god with no power to actually save sinners. Athanasius believed that Christ was not merely like God, he was God and he quoted the Scriptures to prove his case (John 1:1, Col.2:9, 1 Tim.3:16).

But Emperor Constantine was not interested in doctrine and wanted ' peace at any price' in the church. He saw Athanasius as an obstacle to this and so had him banished; in fact during the controversy Athanasius was banned five times, but each time he was recalled. Williston Walker says of him, ' In an age when court favour counted for much, he stood like a rock for his convictions, and that the Nicene theology ultimately conquered was primarily due to him.'[2] As far as Athanasius was concerned the main question was always that of salvation. He saw no hope of this unless Christ was both truly God and man.

Athanasius suffered greatly for his biblical convictions. As well as the five periods of exile, his personal honesty and integrity was continually challenged by the Arians. The pressure on this man of God was so great that he began to feel that it was 'Athanasius against the world.' M. A. Smith says of Athanasius, 'His personal destiny had been inextricably bound up with his wholehearted belief in the full deity of Jesus. He had progressed from the hot-headed zealot to the mature and wise theologian without losing his deeply held convictions. Athanasius died in 373 AD having lived through very difficult times but he bore a faithful witness to the truth of the gospel against all his personal enemies. Although he did not live to see the final victory, it was obvious by the time he died that the decisive battles had been won. Arianism within the Empire was never again a force to be reckoned with, although small groups of Arians existed well into the fifth century.'[3]

Augustine of Hippo

Augustine was born in 354 AD in the ancient city of Tagaste (Thagaste), then in the province of Numidia, North-West Africa but still part of the Roman Empire. This area is now the modern day country of Algeria. His father was a pagan named Patricius but his mother Monica was a devout believer and prayed for her son's conversion from his birth. For a long time these prayers seemed to be unanswered because Augustine lived anything but a Christian life and wrestled with sexual lust. He says in his Confessions, 'From a perverted act of will, desire had grown, and when desire is given satisfaction, habit is forged; and when habit passes unresisted, a compulsive urge sets in.'[4] As he battled with the truths of the gospel the one great barrier to his salvation was this sexual obsession. He wanted to be rid of it but the desire was not that strong; hence his prayer, 'Give me chastity … but not yet.'

At seventeen years old he began living with a young girl but never married her. They had a son named Adeodatus and the girl, although we do not know her name, seems to have helped quell his sexual appetite. His passions moved to reading, especially philosophy, and when he was nineteen he became a professor of rhetoric at Carthage. The reading of Cicero's book *Hortensius* affected him a great deal. He said the book 'changed my affections and turned my prayers to thyself O Lord.'[5] In spite of this claim Augustine was no nearer to knowing God, in fact as he read the Scriptures he said, 'They appeared to me unworthy to be compared with the dignity of Cicero.'[6] He was a man totally wrapped up in the world but not satisfied by it. This is typical of so many who want the best of both worlds.

For nine years his spiritual struggles led him to become a follower of Mani (Manichaeism). This was a sect which believed in a complicated eclectic mix philosophy, superstition, mythology and Christianity. The Christian idea of the Fall and personal sin held no place in Manichaeism for the soul was only evil because of its contact with the physical world which belonged to Satan. Mani saw himself as the last in a long line of prophets which included Jesus. Although Manichaeism was attacked by Christianity it managed to survive in Asia until the 14th Century and elements of it still survive to the present day.

Through the dark years of confusion his mother Monica never ceased to pray for her erring son. At the age of twenty nine he became professor of rhetoric in Milan. He was disillusioned with

Manichaeism but was not yet convinced by Christian doctrine. His conversion came when he was thirty-one. Houghton writes, 'Augustine was in a garden in Milan, weeping and calling to God for deliverance from sin. He despaired of himself. Suddenly he heard the voice of a boy or girl from a neighbouring house repeating in a kind of chant, "Take and read, take and read." Without delay he took up the New Testament and read Romans 13, verses 13-14, the first words on which his eyes fell; "Let us walk honestly, as in the day; not in rioting and drunkenness, not in chambering and wontoness, not in strife and envying. But put ye on the Lord Jesus Christ and make not provision for the flesh to fulfil the lust thereof." Almost at once every shadow of doubt melted away. There and then Augustine passed from death to life. Immediately he went to tell his mother what had happened. She was close at hand, for she had followed him to Italy. Her mourning was now turned into joy, and she blessed the Lord who was able to do exceeding abundantly above all that she had asked or thought.'[7]

While visiting Hippo Augustine was ordained in 391 and became assistant to the elderly bishop Valerius. Four years later, when Valerius died, Augustine became bishop in his own right. He was a deeply spiritual man and very conscious of sin. In his *Confessions* he tells the story of how as a teenager with some friends he stole fruit from a neighbour's pear tree. As he looked back on this incident he could not dismiss it as a childish prank. His serious mind had to find a theological motive for the theft. He thought that perhaps the reason for taking the pears was the thrill of doing something that was wrong.

A man with such strong spiritual convictions is of inestimable worth to the church in any age and particularly in the fifth century when doctrinal controversy was rampant. Augustine was involved in several disputes but probably the most important was Pelagianism

Pelagianism

Pelagius was a British monk who went to Rome around the
year 383. He denied original sin and did not believe the sinner
was helpless to save himself. He also believed that it was possible for a believer to lead a sin-free life; the reward for doing this
was heaven. Houghton describes the teaching of Pelagius as,
'Man is not born sinful, but is able to do all that God requires of
him, if he only wills to do so. Pelagius taught that the ability to
be saved is found in the lost sinners' heart if he will but use it.
He really denied the necessity for a birth from above, for the
inward work of the Holy Spirit, and for the intervention of the
unmerited grace of God.'[8]

Augustine had learnt from his own experience, but more
importantly from the teaching of the Bible, that the sinner needs
grace and without it he has no hope of being acceptable to
God. Pelagianism attacked the heart of the Christian gospel.
Either man can save himself or he can't; either salvation is all of
grace or it is not. There can be no compromise on these questions and Augustine vigorously refused any compromise. His
concept of the greatness of God and the sinfulness of man made
this impossible.

Augustine died in 430 AD during a very troubled time in the
political history of Hippo, but his influence was felt for centuries
after. The Protestant Reformation owes no little debt to this
man. David Wright says, 'The Reformers highlighted different
notes in Augustine. Calvin more thoroughly systematised his
predestinarianism, while Luther was drawn to his grim portrayal
of fallen humanity, probably going beyond Augustine's account
of the bondage of the will … but the kernel of Augustinianism
was everywhere at the heart of the Protestant reformation.'[9]

Like every other man his teaching was not perfect but
Augustine was the greatest Christian of his age. His mind was
at one with the mind of the apostles and he worked to protect
the faith which had been revealed to them.

References

1. N.E.Needham, *2000 years of Christ's Power part 1*. GPT. 2002. p.204.
2. Williston Walker, *History of the Christian Church*. Clark. 1959. p.109.
3. M.A.Smith, *The Church under siege*. IVP. 1976. p.42.
4. Frank James, *Christian History Magazine. Vol. V1. No 3*. p.19.
5. Walker, p.160.
6. *Ibid.*, p.161.
7. S.M.Houghton, *Sketches of Church History.* BOT. 1980. p.25.
8. *Ibid.*, p.27
9. David Wright, *New Dictionary of Theology*. IVP 1988. p.62.

John Wycliffe (1330 [approx] -1384)

(This picture is reproduced by kind permission of David Fountain and is taken from his book 'John Wycliffe - the Dawn of the Reformation.')

Chapter 2
John Wycliffe

John Wycliffe was born in Yorkshire in about the year 1330 when England was in turmoil and spiritual darkness. Little is known about his personal life but we do know that he was a man who was totally taken up with the Word of God and whose incredible mind was to have a great effect in the centuries that followed.

The church dominated medieval life. It was rich in money and property and owned one third of all the land in England. The church was also very corrupt, demanding money from the poor in exchange for pardon from sin. However, although there was plenty of religion, there was no spiritual light. England was poverty stricken in spiritual leadership. To this land came the Black Death in 1348. Bubonic plague started in the East and was borne by rats throughout Europe. It reached England in August of that year and from then on marched in terrifying strides across the country until it reached London. It is variably estimated that between one third and one half of the population died plus a huge number of animals. The whole of the nation ground to a halt and there were not enough left living to bury the dead.

Douglas Wood writes, 'Young Wycliffe escaped unharmed, but to him it seemed like a visit from God – the Judgement Day. So great was his alarm that he spent days and nights on his knees crying to God, repenting and asking God to show him the path that he should follow. When he turned to the Bible (the Vulgate) he found the light and the path that he needed. It was then that he realised how his fellow countrymen were in complete darkness. They had no Bible and most of them could not read Latin, while many could not read at all. A new vision was given to Wycliffe. Some day he would make the Scriptures known to them, too.'[1]

When he was sixteen years old John Wycliffe went to Oxford University. Although he became a great academic scholar with an obvious gift for both learning and teaching, he saw that the Word of God was not something to be learned in the mind only; it had to be acted upon. By the time Wycliffe received his Bachelor of Divinity in 1369 and his Doctorate in 1372 he was regarded as Oxford's leading theologian. He wrote his book *Civil Dominion* at Oxford in which he maintained that the ungodly lose their right to rule if they lead blatantly sinful lives. He applied this teaching to the clergy and said that the secular authorities had the right to confiscate church properties where the clergy were corrupt. This teaching infuriated the bishops but was obviously of interest to secular leaders who wanted to get their hands on the vast wealth of the church.

John of Gaunt

Apart from the King himself, John of Gaunt, the Duke of Lancaster and King Edward III's younger son, was one of the most powerful men in England. The anti-clerical feeling suited his political ambitions and he became a great friend and protector of Wycliffe. On a few occasions this friendship was to save Wycliffe from the wrath of the church authorities. In 1377 Wycliffe was called to London to answer a charge of heresy. John of Gaunt accompanied him to St. Paul's. Merle d'Aubigné describes the scene for us, 'On the 19th February 1377 an immense crowd thronged the approaches to the church and filled its aisles, while the citizens favourable to the reform remained concealed in their houses. Wycliffe moved forward, preceded by Lord Percy, Marshal of England, and supported by the Duke of Lancaster, who defended him for purely political motives. He was followed by four Doctors of Divinity, his counsel, and passed through the hostile multitude ... When the reformer had crossed the threshold of the cathedral, the crowd within appeared like a solid wall; and, not withstanding the efforts of the earl-marshal, Wycliffe and Lancaster could not advance. The people swayed to and fro, hands were raised in violence, and loud hootings re-echoed throughout the building.'[2]

Both Lancaster and Wycliffe were fortunate to escape from St. Paul's with their lives. Three months later the Pope issued charges against Wycliffe listing eighteen errors taught by the reformer. The civil authorities were ordered to hand Wycliffe over to the church but, says Donald Roberts, 'Oxford refused to condemn her outstanding scholar. Instead, Wycliffe consented to a form of house arrest in Black Hall in order to spare the university further punitive action by the Pope. Wycliffe refused to appear again at St. Paul's in the prescribed thirty-day period. He did agree to appear at Lambeth Palace, and in 1378 faced the bishops there. The government still stood by Wycliffe, whose prestige yet ranked high in the land because of the patriotic services he had rendered to the Crown. A message from the Queen Mother [mother of the new young king, Richard II; grandson of Edward III], and the presence of friendly London citizenry were some of the factors which convinced the Commissions of the futility of continuing the trial. They contented themselves with prohibiting Wycliffe from further exposition of his ideas'[3] and again Wycliffe escaped unscathed.

As the reformer's teaching went beyond his political aspirations John of Gaunt came to question Wycliffe's value to him in the political sphere. At the same time the Roman church had problems with two popes seeking to rule at the same time. Rome had enough trouble in this area without bothering too much with a 'heretic' like John Wycliffe.

The Morning Star of the Reformation

D'Aubigné said that if Luther and Calvin were the fathers of the Reformation then Wycliffe was its grandfather. During the last seven years of his life he devoted himself to the teaching of the doctrines that would eventually become crucial to the Reformation – the Church, the Eucharist and the Scriptures.

The Church

Wycliffe not only criticised the corrupted practices of the church but he did something new by attacking the doctrines that gave rise to them. For him the church was the Body of Christ, therefore the only head was Christ himself. The papacy, he said, was an office created by man not God. It was inevitable that from this he would move on to criticise the selling of indulgences. His emphasis was on the individual's personal relationship to God through Christ.

The Eucharist

Transubstantiation – the teaching that the bread and wine of the sacrament is actually turned into the body and blood of Christ in the Mass on being consecrated by the priest – was first accepted by the Roman Catholic church in 1215. To Wycliffe this was not scriptural and from 1379 he repeatedly attacked the doctrine. He called it, 'a blasphemous deceit', and 'a veritable abomination of desolation in the holy places'. Douglas Wood writes, 'Not only was the hierarchy furious at Wycliffe's teaching, but influential friends like Lancaster could not agree with him and follow him down this new path. John stood almost alone, with just a group of his followers at Oxford. He remained firm; he would not yield. In his lectures of 1381 he declared, "The consecrated host we see upon the altar, is neither Christ, nor any part of him, but an effectual sign of him; and that transubstantiation rests upon no scriptural ground."'[4] Wycliffe held to the same doctrine as did Luther, that known as consubstantiation.' (Consubstantiation states that Christ's body and blood are present in the bread and wine but do not replace them).

The Scriptures

Wycliffe's clashes with the church were not due to a contentious spirit but the result of his understanding of scripture. Slowly over a period of time he came more and more to see that the scriptures can be the only authority for what we are to believe. This belief led him inevitably to seeing the need to have the Bible translated into English. All that was available to the church was the Latin Vulgate. If, as Wycliffe said, 'Holy Scripture is the permanent authority for every Christian, and the rule of faith and of all human perfection',[5] then it became of prime importance to have the scriptures in the language of the people. Wycliffe also said, 'For as much as the Bible contains Christ, that is all that is necessary for salvation, it is necessary for all men, nor for priests alone. It alone is the supreme law that is to rule Church, State, and Christian life, without human traditions and statutes.'[6]

Wycliffe and his team of scholars translated the entire Bible from Jerome's Latin Vulgate into the English of his day. The English of the fourteenth century is not the English of today but in looking at Wycliffe's translation of John 3:16 we get a flavour of his work –

> 'Forsothe God so louede the world, that he gaf his oon bigetun sone, that ech man that bileueth in to him perische not, but haue euerlastynge lyf.'

We must remember here that the printing press had still not been invented; every copy of the Bible had to be hand-written. In his book, David Fountain says that 'it has been estimated that it would cost a man six months wages to pay for a New Testament.'[7] There are differing opinions as to the average salary in the UK in the year 2003; but it would mean that the cost of a New Testament would be about £7,500. A staggering amount! For the first time they were available in the English language and ordinary people would buy a few chapters when they could afford them. However the great task of translation was not completed until after Wycliffe's death.

The Lollards

Before the scriptures were translated Wycliffe believed that the best way to reach the people with the gospel was by preaching. He had a high view of preaching and said, 'The highest service to which a man may attain on earth is to preach the law of God. This duty falls peculiarly to priests, in order that they may produce children of God, and this is the end for which God had wedded the church. And for this cause Jesus Christ left other works, and occupied himself mostly in preaching, and thus did the apostles, and on this account God loved them. But now priests are found in taverns and hunting; and playing at their tables, instead of learning God's law and preaching.'[8]

Wycliffe organised a company of laymen to supplement the defective ministry of the clergy. Henry Cowan says, 'The "Poor Priests" lived, like the friars, on Christian alms, but preached evangelical doctrine based entirely on Holy Writ. Personally trained by Wycliffe himself, they travelled about bare-foot, in long gowns of coarse cloth, preaching in church or church yard, when permitted, and also at market of fair.'[9] David Fountain calls them 'his Bible Men'. These men came to be known as Lollards although it is not known the exact meaning of the name. It can be a term of abuse meaning 'one who mumbles or mutters' or a 'tare' (sown among wheat) or it may come from the German 'lollen' – to sing with a low voice. They never stayed long in one place but however much these men where hounded they kept on preaching the gospel and spoke to all who would listen to them; lord and labourer alike. The Lollards, far from dying out, established congregations all over England and Scotland. Although they continued to be hounded as heretics they continued right up until the Reformation.

Wycliffe was not a well man and spent the last days of his life at his home in Lutterworth. He died on December 31st 1384 after a series of strokes. Over thirty years after his death the Council of Constance in Bavaria branded Wycliffe's writings as heretical and ordered his books and his bones to be burnt. But it was not until 1427 that his remains were dug up and burned and the ashes cast into the river Swift. David Fountain says 'and his ashes were to be disposed of so that no trace of him should be seen again'.[10] Thomas Fuller, the church historian of the 17th century, wrote, 'the brook Swift did carry his ashes into the Avon, and the Avon into the Severn, then the Severn into the narrow seas, then into the main ocean; and thus the ashes of Wycliffe are emblems of his doctrine, which is now diffused over all the world.'[11]

Reformation

D'Aubigné says, 'Wycliffe is the greatest of English reformers …
in many respects Wycliffe is the Luther of England.'[12] Wycliffe
is often called 'the morning star of the Reformation'. His beliefs
spread to Europe, and especially to Bohemia. The Reformation, the great movement of God that changed the hearts and
beliefs of so many theologians, itself has had a vast amount
written about it. But do not think of the 'Dark Ages', the period
before the Reformation, as being without any light at all. Men
like John Wycliffe opened the way for the true 'Great Light' to
shine and had great influence on the centuries to come.

References

1. Douglas Wood, *The Evangelical Doctor.* EP 1984. p.10.
2. Merle d'Aubigné, *Reformation in England.* BOT 1962. p.83.
3. Donald Roberts, *Christian History. Vol 1. No 2.* p.12.
4. Douglas Wood, p.84.
5. Donald Roberts, p.13
6. *Ibid.,* p.26.
7. David Fountain, *John Wycliffe - the Dawn of the Reformation.* Mayflower Christian Books 1984. p.49.
8. Donald Roberts, p.24.
9. Henry Cowan, *Landmarks of Church history.* Black 1894. p.121.
10. David Fountain, p.72.
11. Henry Cowan, p.124.
12. Merle d'Aubigné, p.98.

Martin Luther (1483-1546)

Chapter 3
Martin Luther

Martin Luther was born on November 10th 1483 at Eisleben in Germany. He said he was the son of a peasant which was true, but his father Hans worked hard and came eventually to own several copper mines. Martin's parents wanted him to become a lawyer and he entered university with that aim. He earned both his bachelors and masters degrees very quickly, but his whole course of life was changed in 1505 when he was caught in a frightening thunderstorm. He was terrified when a bolt of lightening struck the ground near him and in fear cried out to the patron saint of miners, 'Help me, Saint Anne [the patroness of miners] I will become a monk.'[1]

It would have been easy and perhaps understandable, if once the danger of the thunderstorm was over, Luther had forgotten his vow and got on with his life. But he kept his vow and in July 1505 entered a monastery of the Black Cloister of the Observant Augustinians. With typical enthusiasm he threw himself into his new life and later said, 'If anyone could have earned heaven by the life of a monk, it was I.'[2]

The monastery brought no peace to Luther and he was plagued with a deep sense of sin. He did as the Roman Catholic Church prescribed and confessed his sin in the sacrament of confession. James Kittelson writes, 'But Luther knew that in the midst of this most crucial act, he was at his most selfish. He was confessing his sins and performing his penance out of the intensely human instinct to save his own skin. Yet because of the human tendency to sin, one could hardly confess enough. This critical issue remained vivid in Luther's mind.'[3] He commented later, 'If one were to confess his sins in a timely manner, he would have to carry a confessor in his pocket!' As his teachers knew, this fact could lead to despair. In Luther's case it occasionally did.'[4]

He struggled with a terrible sense of guilt. Roland Bainton says, 'Luther's question was not whether his sins were big or little, but whether they had been confessed. The great difficulty which he encountered was to be sure that everything had been recalled. He learnt from experience the cleverness of memory in protecting the ego, and he was frightened when after six hours of confessing he could still go out and think of something else which had eluded his most conscientious scrutiny. Still more disconcerting was the discovery that some of man's misdemeanours are not even recognised, let alone remembered.'[5]

Saving Truth

Luther continued in this spiritual wilderness for several years. He sought God but found no comfort; in fact he was increasingly terrified by the wrath of God. By now he was teaching theology in Wittenberg and it was the study of the Bible that was to bring light to his soul.

One particular verse was a great problem to him – Romans 1:17, *'For in the gospel a righteousness from God is revealed, a righteousness that is by faith from first to last, just as it is written, "The righteous will live by faith."'* 'He thought', says S. M. Houghton, 'these words refer to the awful holiness of God, and his unchanging hatred of sin and sinners. How could he, Martin Luther, ever achieve the kind of holiness that would turn away the anger of God against him? He did not yet understand Paul's words in Romans that the gospel is the saving power of God to everyone who believes in Christ because it reveals the right-eousness of God. This righteousness of God is nothing other than Christ's perfect obedience to his Father's will in life and death, even the death of the cross – obedience which God counts as belonging to all those in whose place Christ died. Just as the punishment of the believer's sin was borne by Christ so it is because of Christ's righteousness that the same believer, though ungodly in himself, is pronounced just or righteous in the sight of God.'[6]

When, by the grace of God, Luther came to believe this truth, that *'The just shall live by faith,'* a personal reformation came to him. This had to happen before God used him in the great Reformation that shook Europe. God brought saving truth to Martin Luther by the very verse which was his great stum-bling block. He said, 'I felt as if I were entirely born again and had entered paradise itself through gates that had been flung open.'[7]

Once this truth came to him, it was far more than under-standing one Bible verse. The whole Bible was now seen in a different light and the peace and comfort he had so long sought now filled his soul. When he lectured on Psalm 22 Luther came to a new view of God and Christ; a view that contradicted all his church stood for. It was inevitable that when a man such as Martin Luther saw these things, sooner or later there would be a spiritual explosion that would shake the whole world.

Indulgences

Indulgences guaranteed release from purgatory after a certain number of years. They were documents sold by the church to

individuals for themselves or on behalf of dead relatives which
Loraine Boettner says, 'This release from punishment is said to
be possible because the church has a vast treasury of unused
merits which have been accumulated primarily through the
suffering of Christ but also because of the good works of Mary
and the saints who have done works more perfect than God's
law requires for their own salvation. Thus not only the suffering
and death of Christ, but also the good works of Mary and the
saints, are the grounds of forgiveness of sins. The church claims
to be able to withdraw merits from that store and apply them to
any member of the church just as if he had suffered what was
necessary for the forgiveness of sins.'[8] For obvious reasons these
documents were highly sought after and were the means of
raising a great deal of money for the church. Whenever money
was needed to build a cathedral, this was the way it was raised.
Indulgences were the lottery of the 16th century.

In 1570 Pope Leo X wanted a great deal of money to
continue building Saint Peter's Basilica in Rome. To get this
money he extended the sale of indulgences. A monk named
Tetzel came near to Wittenberg selling indulgences on behalf of
the pope. Tetzel was a born salesman and excited great public
attention. He had a commodity for sale that appealed to the
superstitious minds of people who knew nothing of divine grace
and he encouraged their superstition with the jingle – 'Once the
coin into the coffer clings, a soul from purgatory heavenward
springs.'

Houghton tells us that, 'Luther's anger was unbounded. He
preached vehemently against Tetzel and his ecclesiastical wares,
but soon decided to take more vigorous action, for men in
general had no conscience against purchasing indulgences which
guaranteed the remission of purgatorial pains. Luther, therefore, wrote 95 theses, tersely stating the evils of indulgences;
and on the 31st of October 1517, at the hour of noon, he nailed
them to the door of the Castle Church at Wittenberg. This was
the beginning of the Reformation.'[9]

The 95 Theses

At first Luther did not attack the *idea* of indulgences, his objection was to their *abuse* as demonstrated by Tetzel. But the *idea* lent itself inevitably to *abuse* and the question soon became, 'did the pope have the right to issue indulgences?' At that point the authority of the church was in question.

The 95 theses consisted of brief statements Luther made concerning indulgences. Here are some of them...

• 27   They preach human folly who pretend that as soon as money in the coffer rings a soul from purgatory springs.
• 32   Those who suppose that on account of their letters of indulgence they are sure of salvation will be eternally damned along with their teachers.
• 37   Every true Christian, whether living or dead, has a share in all the benefits of Christ and the Church, for God has granted him these, even without letters of indulgence.
• 45   Christians should be taught that whoever sees a person in need, and instead of helping him, uses his money for an indulgence, obtains not an indulgence from the pope but the displeasure of God.
• 51   Christians should be taught that the pope ought and should give his own substance to the poor, from whom certain preachers of indulgences extract money, even if he had to sell St. Peter's Cathedral to do it.
• 81   This shameless preaching of pardons makes it hard even for learned men to defend the pope's honour against calumny or to answer the indubitable questions of laity.
• 82   For example; Why does not the pope empty purgatory for the sake of holy love... for after all, he does release countless souls for the sake of sordid money contributed for the building of a cathedral?

- 94   We should admonish Christians to follow Christ, their head, through punishment, death and hell.
- 95   And so let them set their trust on entering heaven through many tribulations rather than some false security and peace.

These were soon read, copied, printed and distributed all over Germany and eventually the whole of Europe.

The Pope Retaliates

At first the pope did not treat the matter seriously and dismissed it as a monk's squabble but he quickly changed his mind and demanded that Luther come to Rome. Luther refused because he knew that this would have meant certain death. The pope then sent Cardinal Cajetan to Germany to deal with the reformer. Attempts were made to slacken the support Frederick the Wise, Elector of Saxony, had been giving to Luther. All this failed and the pope finally excommunicated him.

Previously Luther, like all members of the Roman church, had accepted the supreme authority of the pope, but when he began to examine more carefully the basis for this authority he was appalled to discover it rested on forged documents. Houghton writes, 'Two famous documents, both of them forgeries, further assisted the growth of the power of the papacy. The so-called Donation of Constantine claimed that the Emperor of that name, when he went to live at Byzantium, had granted the bishops of Rome very extensive rights in Italy, including the privilege of wearing a golden crown. Later, documents called the Decretals, professing to be letters and decrees of bishops of Rome going back to apostolic days, exalted the powers of the church in general, and assisted the bishops of Rome to establish their authority in both Church and State.'[10]

Since the 15th century scholars had known that the Decretals were false but this did not seem to make any difference to the power the church gave the pope. However it made a great deal of difference to Martin Luther. He declared that the authority of the pope was unknown in scripture and freed himself from this authority. The result of this, says Renwick, was that 'he seemed now to have the strength of a hundred men and poured forth a constant stream of sermons and pamphlets through the printing presses.'[11]

Emperor Charles V entered the fray and ordered Luther to appear before him in the city of Worms. Friends of Luther tried to persuade him not to go but his famous reply was, 'If there are as many devils in Worms as tiles on the housetops I will still go.' He arrived there on April 16th 1521 to be questioned by a former friend named John Eck. Dr. Eck demanded that Luther should withdraw his books to which the reformer answered, 'Unless I am convinced by testimonies of the Scriptures or by clear arguments that I am in error – for popes and councils have often erred and contradicted themselves – I cannot withdraw, for I am subject to the Scriptures I have quoted; my conscience is captive to the Word of God. It is unsafe and dangerous to do anything against one's conscience. Here I stand; I cannot do otherwise. So help me God.'[12]

This was too much for the church authorities and the reformer was condemned. Fortunately he had an assurance of safe conduct to Worms so he left quickly. In order to save his life the Elector of Saxony sent a group of men to convey him to safety on the way home. He was taken to Wartburg Castle and spent nearly a year there. His enemies thought he was dead but at Wartburg he translated the New Testament into German – a work of great importance for the Reformation.

Luther and the Reformers

Luther was not the only reformer God raised up during the Reformation. Zwingli, Calvin and many others all paid a prominent part in turning the church back to a biblical faith. These were all men intensely concerned about doctrine. Luther was by nature an angry man. He said, 'Anger refreshes all my blood, sharpens my mind and drives away temptations.'[13] Obviously he saw anger as a strength but unfortunately it made it difficult for him to see viewpoints other than his own. This was particularly true concerning differences over the Lord's Supper. Renwick says, 'Luther believed in consubstantiation, i.e. That Christ was present bodily in the bread and wine and asserted that the words "This is my body" must be taken literally. Zwingli, the Swiss leader, held that the bread and wine were only signs which reminded men of the sacrifice of Christ, and that they fed on him by faith. Luther was immovable and bitter. His intransigence caused incalculable loss to the Protestant cause.'[14]

On October 1ˢᵗ 1529 the reformers met at Martburg to discuss their differences. This conference lasted for three days and came to an agreement on 14 out of 15 points under discussion. Predictably it was the Lord's Supper that was the sticking point. The controversy was bitter. Luther said, 'One side in this controversy belongs to the Devil and is God's enemy.'[15]

John Calvin was younger than Luther and the two men never met, but there was not the same animosity between these two reformers. In fact Luther said, 'I might have entrusted the whole of this controversy to him from the beginning.' He felt that, 'If my opponents had done the like, we would soon have been reconciled.'[16] Whether this was realistic is open to doubt for Luther condemned all who disagreed with him as enemies of the Reformation.'

Evangelicals who did not always agree with Luther were not so unkind in their language. They acknowledged how greatly God had used him but did not believe that he was always right either in his doctrine or manner. Most of the other reformers would have agreed with Calvinist Theodore Beza, who proclaimed in 1580 that Luther's work 'resulted in the cleansing of God's sanctuary, delivering it from the clutches of the Antichrist at an opportune moment, and he used the Word of God as a means of returning it to the Lordship of Christ... Luther was a man with faults and with turbulent disciples, but still a great man,'[17] He adhered firmly to the biblical doctrine of 'Justification by faith' and this became the battle cry of the Reformation. After years of ill health he died in the town of his birth, Eisleben, in 1546.

References

1. James Kittleton, *Christian History. Vol X1 No 2.* p.10.
2. *Ibid.,* p.11.
3. *Ibid.,* p.12
4. *Ibid.,* p.12
5. Roland Bainton, *Here I Stand.* Menton 1978. p.41.
6. S.M.Houghton, *Sketches of Church History* BOT. p.81.
7. James Kittleton, p.15.
8. Loraine Boettner, *Roman Catholicism.* BOT. 1966. p.337.
9. S.M.Houghton, p.85.
10. *Ibid*, p.32.
11. A.M.Renwick, *The Story of the church.* IVP 1958. p.114.
12. S.M.Houghton, p.89.
13. James Kittleton, p.10.
14. A.M.Renwick, p.114.
15. Robert Linder, *Christian History. Vol X11 No.3* p.42.
16. *Ibid.,* p.44.
17. *Ibid.,* p.44

William Tyndale (1495 -1536)

Chapter 4
William Tyndale

In chapter 2 we read how John Wycliffe was the first man to translate the Bible into the language of the English people, using as his translation the Latin Vulgate. This was done before the invention of printing so each copy had to be hand written and this clearly limited its popular use. It was not until 1526, some 200 years later, that William Tyndale translated from the original Greek and the first ever New Testament in English was printed mechanically. Tyndale's desire was that the English ploughboy would be able to read the scriptures and printing obviously went a long way to making this possible.

So mechanically, events favoured Tyndale's work but he still had the vicious opposition of the Catholic Church. In 1519 the church publicly burned a woman and six men for nothing more than teaching their children the English version of the Lord's Prayer and Ten Commandments. Tyndale was to experience the same fate and at the age of 42 years he was strangled and burned at the stake for translating the Bible into English.

William Tyndale was born some time between 1493 and 1495. He gained his MA at Oxford in 1515 and afterwards moved to Cambridge. It was probably at Cambridge that he was first introduced to Protestant doctrines. He had a keen mind and a gift for languages. However he was no admirer of the way universities taught theology. Later he wrote, 'In the universities they have ordained that no man shall look on the

Scripture until he be nozzled in heathen learning 8 or 9 years, and armed with false principles with which he is clean shut out of the understanding of the Scripture.'[1]

It was the time of the Renaissance. For years the universities of Oxford and Cambridge (the only two universities at that time) had been in decline. But things were changing. Men were beginning to question the status quo. 'The revival of learning and culture, literature and art were establishing their importance in men's minds ... Behind it all was an unseen hand preparing England for the greatest reformation she would ever receive.'[2]

In 1521 William joined the household of Sir John Walsh at Little Sodbury Manor in Gloucester, either as chaplain or tutor to the children. Here he had plenty of time for study and meditation. Tony Lane tells us, 'many of the local clergy came to dine at the Walsh's Manor, which gave Tyndale ample opportunity both to be shocked by their ignorance of the Bible and to become embroiled in controversy with them. To one such cleric he declared; 'If God spare my life, ere many years pass, I will cause a boy that driveth the plough shall know more of the Scripture than thou dost.'[3]

London

In 1523 Tyndale went to London to seek the support of Bishop Tunstall for his desire to translate the Bible. Tunstall refused to help and Brian Edwards says, 'Tyndale was cast down, but not destroyed. He had tried to translate the New Testament legally and had been refused. But the man behind the plough would have the Scriptures in a plain language – somehow. Years later in 1540 when the Great Bible was issued, bearing most of the work of Tyndale between its pages, Tunstall's name appeared on the title page, authorising it! There are always fearful and accommodating men who revel in the liberty gained by the blood of others.'[4]

In London Tyndale met a rich merchant named Humphrey Monmouth. A warm friendship developed between the two men and Monmouth welcomed Tyndale in his home for six months. Tyndale preached regularly in London. D'Aubigné writes, 'The Word of God was with him the basis of salvation, and the grace of God its essence. His inventive mind presented the truths he proclaimed in a striking manner.'[5]

Tyndale and Luther

Though preaching was important to him, Tyndale believed his main ministry was to translate the scriptures into English. But it was clear that the printing could not be done in England so in 1524 he moved to Germany and in Hamburg worked on his translation of the New Testament. This was ready to be printed in 1525.

By the spring of 1524 Tyndale had moved to Wittenburg. It would have been amazing if he did not meet up with Martin Luther there and although Luther does not mention a meeting, it almost certainly took place. The two great reformers were involved in the same task of translating the scriptures into their respective native languages. In many ways it would have been safer for the English man to have stayed in Wittenburg but he remained there for only nine months. Brian Edwards says, 'One of the most pressing reasons why Tyndale left the security of Luther's university was simply that he did not wish to become a Lutheran. Even the translations and traces of Luther in his work reveal Tyndale's strength and independence of character. Where he felt the German reformer had well expressed a particular position, Tyndale saw no need to waste his own words upon it. This was not plundering another's work unjustly, for many of his readers would readily recognise the source, as Sir Thomas Moore certainly did, and Tyndale openly admitted his love for Luther and ran often to his defence when Moore attacked him. However, Tyndale often altered what Luther had written, and added his own contribution, if he felt he had some better way of expressing the issue. And, of course, the greater proportion of Tyndale's work both in original writing and in translation, is all his own and reveals his complete independence of mind. He was a slave to no man's thoughts.'[6]

Printing

The first English New Testament was printed in Cologne but a raid by the authorities on the press forced Tyndale to flee. Only one incomplete copy of the Cologne New Testament still survives. He moved to Worms and 6,000 copies were printed but only two of these survived to the present day. The reason so few of the early additions have survived is that the English New Testament was banned in England. Dr. Tony Lane says, 'They were smuggled into England and the bishops did all they could to eradicate them. In 1526 none other than Cuthbert Tunstall preached against the translation and had copies ceremoniously burned at St. Paul's. The following year the archbishop of Canterbury had the idea of himself buying up copies of the New Testament in order to destroy them.'[7]

The opposition could not prevent copies getting to the people Tyndale intended to reach with the Word of God. Although it took half a week's wages to buy a copy, this did not prevent a ready sale. Poor people would buy a New Testament between them and share their precious new possession.

The Translation

It is no exaggeration to call Tyndale 'The father of the English Bible.' What he accomplished was to have a great effect on all following translations and even upon the English language. Edwards says, 'So great was the influence of his revised edition of 1534 that many of its spellings became the accepted norm. It is rarely appreciated how heavily dependent upon Tyndale was every translation of the Scriptures up to, and including, the Authorised Version of King James. A full ninety per cent of the Authorised Version of the New Testament stands virtually unaltered from Tyndale's 1534 revision (spelling excepted) and at least seventy five per cent of the Revised Version likewise.'[8]

Here is Tyndale's translation of the opening verses of 1 Corinthians 13 –

> Though I speake with the tonges of men and angels/and yet had no love/I were even as soundynge brasse: and as a tynklynge Cynball. and though I coulde prophesy/and vnderstode all secretes/and all knowledge:yee/if I had all fayth so I coulde move mountayns oute of there places/and yet had no love/I were nothynge. And though I bestowed all my gooddes to fede the poore/and though I gave my body even that I burned/and yet have no love/it profeteth me nothynge.

Betrayal and Death

The more copies of the New Testament which entered England, the greater was the anger of the church authorities. Their determination to put the translator to death increased to such an extent that by 1533 agents were hunting Tyndale all over the continent. One of these agents was Henry Phillips, a man in desperate need of money who was really working for one of the bishops in England. He arrived in Antwerp and began with charm and guile to infiltrate the company of the English merchants who were Tyndale's supporters. He met Tyndale and was warmly received. Phillips gained all the information he needed about Tyndale and then left for Brussels to seek the help of the court in arresting Tyndale. He returned to Antwerp with a small group of officers and proceeded to lay an ambush to capture the translator.

Tyndale was arrested and taken to the castle of Vilvoorde, north of Brussels, to await trial. Inevitably he was found guilty of heresy and in October 1536 he was strangled and then his body was burned at the stake. A true martyr for the sake of the gospel.

The following year Henry VIII encouraged the distribution of Miles Coverdale's English Bible among the people. This translation was mostly Tyndale's work unaltered. And in 1539 the King of England encouraged all printers to provide for the 'free and liberal use of the Bible in our own maternal English tongue'.

References

1. Donald Roberts, *Christian History Vol V1 No. 4.* p.6.
2. Brian Edwards. *God's Outlaw*, EP 1999. p.31.
3. Tony Lane, *Christian History, Vol VI No. 4.* pp.6-7
4. Brian Edwards, p.67.
5. D'Aubigné, *Reformation in England.* BOT 1962. p.191.
6. Brian Edwards, p.80.
7. Tony Lane, *Great Leaders of the Christian Church.* Moody 1988. p. 203.
8. Brian Edwards, p.102.

Oliver Cromwell (1599-1658)

Chapter 5
Oliver Cromwell

Oliver Cromwell was born on April 25th 1599 to Robert and Elizabeth Cromwell of Huntingdon. Cromwell described his early years, 'I was by birth a gentleman, living neither in any considerable height nor yet in obscurity.'[1] Though they were not a wealthy family, they had a high pedigree in that Henry VIII's chief minister Thomas Cromwell was Oliver's great, great, great uncle. In fact Oliver owed his surname to the pride the family had in Thomas Cromwell's reputation. Oliver's side of the family were not strictly Cromwells at all, but Williams and Oliver's marriage contract had him named, 'alias Williams'.

He was educated at Huntingdon grammar school where he came under the influence of Dr. Thomas Beard. Antonia Fraser describes Beard – 'In broad terms, and in so far as labels can be helpfully used, he might be described as a striking example of the sort of men, intellectual, proselytizing, courageous, above all determined to sort out honestly the relationship of God to man, and the correct part to be played in this by the Church, who made up the body of early English Puritans.'[2]

Cromwell went to Cambridge in 1616 but left in 1617 on the death of his father. His formal education was completed with three years at the Inns of Court in London. In 1620 he married Elizabeth Bourchier and in 1628, at the age of 29, he became MP for Huntingdon. This was in the third year of the reign of Charles 1st.

From the beginning King Charles had been at variance with Parliament, one reason being that the MPs refused to give him all the money and supplies he demanded. To counteract this the King forced a levy of £300,000 and those who refused to pay were imprisoned. Judges were dismissed for denying the legality of the forced loan and church ministers were promoted for declaring it sinful to refuse payment. The situation in England was getting exceedingly stormy. War with France and Spain forced Charles to call his third parliament in 1628 in the hope of raising more money. His financial situation was desperate and this gave Parliament the opportunity to force the King to accept the 'Petition of Rights'. This famous document declared that arbitrary imprisonment and taxation without the consent of Parliament was to be hence forth illegal. The King with great reluctance was forced to accept.

The quarrel between King and Parliament was not only about politics and money, religion also played a crucial part. In November 1628 Charles issued a Declaration which was prefixed to the Book of Common Prayer. This was resented greatly by the Puritans because they saw in it the strong papalism of Archbishop Laud, the King's new favourite. As things went from bad to worse Cromwell became increasingly opposed to the King.

The situation came to a head in 1629. Fraser says, 'On 2nd March Cromwell was among those who refused to adjourn at the King's command until the resolution of Sir John Eliot condemning popery and illegal subsidies not granted by parliament was passed... By the time King Charles succeeded in dissolving parliament, thus drawing to an end parliamentary government in England for the next eleven years, the damage was done and the resolutions had been read. Perhaps it was Oliver's first sight of a short sharp physical action in a righteous cause.'[3]

Conversion

Oliver Cromwell was by birth, family background and education, a strong Protestant but he was not yet a born-again Christian. Exactly when he was converted we are not sure but it followed a period of intense inward and spiritual turmoil beginning about 1628. Some have dismissed this period as a nervous breakdown but a friend of Cromwell, who could see the great spiritual battle that was going on, wrote many years later, 'This great man is risen from a very low and afflicted condition; one that hath suffered very great troubles of soul, lying a long time under sore terrors and temptations, and at the same time in a very low condition for outward things; in this school of affliction he was kept, till he had learned the lesson of the Cross, till his will was broken into submission to the will of God. Religion was thus laid into his soul with the hammer and fire; it did not come in only by light into his understanding.'[4]

In 1638 Cromwell wrote in a letter to his cousin, 'You know what my manner of life hath been. Oh, I lived in and loved darkness, and hated light; I was a chief, the chief of sinners. This is true, I hated godliness, yet God had mercy on me ... yet the Lord forsaketh me not. Though he do prolong, yet he will I trust bring me to his tabernacle, to his resting-place. My soul is with the Congregation of the First- born, my body rests in hope... He giveth me to see light in his light.'[5]

This is surely the language of a soul that delights in the love and grace of God. This was now a man of God, a man of deep faith and a man of the Bible. For the rest of his life, whether in great affairs of state or in times of personal crisis, his strength came from the word of God. In 1658, at the death of his daughter Bettie and finding himself deeply distressed, he read aloud from the Bible, 'I have learnt in that whatever state I am, therewith to be content. I know how to be debased and I know how to abound. I can do all things through Christ that strengtheneth me.' Then he said, 'This scripture did once save my life, when my eldest son died, which went as a dagger to my heart.'[6]

The Short Parliament

Between the years of 1629 and 1640 there was no parliament and a bitterness grew in the whole country. To add to this in 1630 and 1631 the harvests were bad and poverty was rife. The Puritan cause seemed doomed. One Puritan lawyer wrote, 'All our liberties were now at once utterly ruined.' Many of the Puritans turned increasingly towards the colonies in the New World to escape the frustrations of royal or episcopal control. Cromwell himself seems to have seriously considered emigrating with his family to America in the early 1630s.

In the year 1638 the turning point in the history of English Puritanism came via Scotland and the Covenanters. When it began, the King's power seemed as firmly established as his heart could desire. But for all his Stuart blood, Charles I had never understood or liked Scotland and the feeling was mutual. Several events led up to the First Bishops War between England and Scotland, – extremely heavy taxation, the popish overtones in the coronation service and the publishing of the new liturgy for Scotland in 1637 with a prefix that its use was demanded by royal command. In March 1638 the Scots took the Covenant and the little cloud in the north became a threatening storm.

Early in 1640 the King was compelled, because of the wastage of money in the Scottish war, to recall parliament. This was known as the 'Short Parliament' and only lasted a few weeks. The war with Scotland was useless, the country and the army had no use for it. So in November 1640, with Scottish army camped on English soil, the 'Long Parliament' met. It was now, at the age of 41, that Cromwell began to come to the political forefront.

The Long Parliament

In the twenty two months from the beginning of the 'Long Parliament' to the outbreak of the Civil War, Cromwell became more and more passionately involved in the affairs of Parliament. He sat on numerous committees concerned with all sort of affairs but pre-eminently he was absorbed in the matter of state and church. Though not yet completely convinced of Independency he was soon to emerge as one of the leading Independents. If this particular conviction was still developing, his anti-episcopalian views were already fully developed. In 1641 he strongly supported, 'An Act for the abolishing of superstition and idolatry, and for the better advancing of the true worship and service of God.' This obviously was strongly resented by the Anglican Church, to which Cromwell answered, 'he was more convinced touching the irregularity of Bishops than ever before, because, like the Roman hierarchy, they would not endure to have their condition come to trial.'[7]

This was followed soon after by the 'Root and Branch Bill'. This proposed to do away with bishops altogether and took its name from an earlier petition demanding the abolition of episcopacy 'with all its dependencies, roots and branches'. This bill was later abandoned but the House did pass some very basic Puritan beliefs – forbidding sports on the Lord's Day, forbidding bowing at the name of Jesus and the removal of pictures of the Trinity and the Virgin Mary from churches. On September 8th of that year a motion was passed, which Cromwell had personally introduced, to the effect that sermons should be preached in the afternoons in all parishes of England. This was a direct reversal of Archbishop Laud's policy.

The year 1641 was a crucial one leading up to the Civil War and two events were of vital importance. In August the King went to Scotland to seek to use one kingdom against the other. But more importantly in October the Irish rebelled. Thus these two events, the growing distrust of Charles and the great fear of popery in Ireland, inflamed an already heated Parliament.

The Irish rebellion and the stories of the horrific massacres had great repercussions, particularly eight years later when Cromwell's armies took its revenge. The stories coming into England from Ulster of the massacre of the English settlers were greatly exaggerated but they were believed. Fraser says, 'in considering the climate of English opinion at this date, which is of extreme importance in the case of Oliver Cromwell who stands permanently arraigned at the bar of humanity for his actions against the Irish eight years later, the salient point is not whether the massacres took place or not, but whether they were believed to have taken place in England at the time. Here the evidence is unanimous; it was an article of faith among English Protestants that this wicked, inhuman slaughter of innocent women and children, with a strong overtone of a Catholic Holy War, had raged through Ireland.'[8] It was believed that the Irish Catholics had killed something like 200,000 Protestants.

News of all this arrived in London on November 1st, the day in which Parliament was to discuss the Great Remonstrance. This was an enormous attack on the position of the monarchy and was so crucial that Cromwell said that if the Remonstrance were rejected he would immediately emigrate to the New World. It was passed by the Commons on November 22nd but although the lines were set, it would be another eight months before the Civil War began. Up to this time Cromwell was not considered to be one of the leaders of the Parliamentary party but his reputation was growing. In July the King sent soldiers to Cambridge to get the university's silver plate. Cromwell, as MP for the town, with his followers marched on King's College with drums beating and flags flying to ensure that any treasure there went to Parliament and not the King. Cromwell was successful and £20,000 was saved for Parliament.

On August 22nd 1642 Charles raised his standard at Nottingham and the Civil War began. Fraser says, 'Although the contestants had at the time believed they were fighting for liberty, to make Parliament the supreme trustee of the law in England, another cause had finally emerged – the manner of the worship of God.'[9]

Civil War

In 1642 England was quite unprepared for a Civil War. There was no army as such and very few English men had experience of leadership in battle. It was a war of the amateur soldier and Cromwell was very aware that the parliamentary forces were anything but ready for the strife. Many of them were still unsure if it was lawful to fight the King. The confusion of mind was so acute that the wording of the Parliament commission to raise a troop declared that the men should be ready to fight 'for King and Parliament'. Cromwell was impatient with this attitude and declared bluntly that if the King happened to be in the midst of the ranks of the enemy as he charged that he would fire at the King as at any other individual.

Cromwell started the war as a captain but by January 1644 he was Lieutenant General and second in command to the Earl of Manchester. He continually disagreed with Manchester's reluctance to press the battle to the enemy and grew very frustrated with Manchester's inability to grasp the importance of a victory on the battlefield. Manchester, like many of the parliamentary leaders, did not believe that the only way to victory was through war. This attitude and reluctance to press the battle really prolonged the war. One authority believes that if Manchester had seized his chance after the victory of Marston Moor in 1644 the war could have been over by the end of the year.

Cromwell was not only unhappy with the leadership but also with the troops of Parliament. After the first battle at Edgehill he said to Hampden, 'Your troops are most of them old decayed servingmen and tapsters and such kind of fellows; and their troupers (Royalists) are gentlemen's sons, persons of quality; do you think that the spirits of such base and mean fellows will be ever able to encounter gentlemen that have honour and courage and resolution in them.'[10]

This led to him forming eventually the 'New Model Army', which in turn sprang from a deeply held conviction of the potential superiority of the godly in terms of worldly success as well as spiritual salvation. Fraser tells us that Richard Baxter said Cromwell 'had a special care to get religious men into his troop because these were the sort of men he esteemed and loved; and although this was his original motive, naturally from this happy and worthy choice flowed the avoidings of those disorders, mutinies, plunderings and grievances of the country which debased men in armies are commonly guilty of.'[11]

Cromwell sought to get chaplains to minister to his soldiers and Baxter was invited to become pastor to the officers, but he declined this. Fraser described the moral quality of these soldiers – 'from the first the discipline of troops in their private habits was in marked contrast to the general run of military custom ... By May the Parliamentarian newspaper Special Passages recorded with approval that Colonel Cromwell had "2,000 brave men, well disciplined; no man swears but he pays his twelve pence; if he be drunk he is set in the stocks, or worse, if one calls the other Roundhead he is cashiered; in so much that the countries where they come leap for joy of them, and come in and join with them."'[12]

The conflict between Cromwell and Manchester led to passing the 'Self Denying Ordinance', which meant that within forty days all MPs had to relinquish their commands in the army. This effectively made Cromwell no longer a soldier, only a politician, but his reputation as a cavalry officer forced him back into the fighting. A series of brilliant victories ensured that he alone of all the parliamentary leaders stayed an MP and soldier. He was absolutely convinced that God was leading him. He wrote in a battle report, 'I hope you will pardon me if I say, God is not enough owned. We look too much to men and visible helps.'[13] The Battle of Naseby in 1645 underlines Cromwell's sense of God with him. He wrote a month after the battle, 'I can say this of Naseby, when I saw the enemy draw up and march in gallant order towards us, and we a company of poor, ignorant men, to seek out to order our battle – the General having commanded me to order all the horse – I could not, riding alone about my business, but smile out to God in praises, in assurance of victory, because God would, by things that are not, bring to naught things that are. Of which I had great assurance, and God did it.'[14]

After Naseby the King's position, both from a military and a political point of view, was hopeless. Letters captured showed that Charles was negotiating with the Duke of Lorraine to send 10,000 troops to England. Neutral Englishmen turned now to Parliament. By June 24th 1646 the war was virtually over and Cromwell returned to his duties in Parliament.

Conflict in Parliament

During the Civil War the parliamentary side had its own internal conflicts between the Presbyterians and the Independents. In Parliament the Independents were a minority yet the army was a stronghold of Independency. The confusion and tension was enormous. Parliament disbanded the army and refused to pay the wages owed to the soldiers. By April 1647 the army was ready for mutiny. All this time King Charles was a prisoner of the Scots.

Cromwell was sent to try and sort out the mess and for a while it seemed that his conciliatory efforts might work. But Parliament was determined to disband the army and impose Presbyterianism on England, even if it meant bringing in the Scottish army to enforce it. It meant a new civil war. Cromwell joined in with the side of the army and struck with swiftness and decision. The King, now back in England, was the key to the position and Cromwell set out to capture him. An interview between Cromwell and Charles on July 4th went so well that many believed that an understanding between King and army could be reached within fourteen days. Cromwell was even prepared to allow religious freedom to the Catholics. But all the time Charles was also scheming with the Scots, and with an almost mad arrogance he rejected Cromwell's advances.

On August 6th 1647 the army marched in triumph into London. Fairfax was still the commanding officer but Cromwell was now the undisputed political leader.

The Kings Execution

There was a deep division among the Parliamentarians as to what to do with the King. Cromwell made his position very clear when on October 20th 1647 he made a strong speech in the Commons in support of the monarchy. He spoke very favourably of Charles, concluding it was necessary to re-establish him as soon as possible. What he wished to see was a very much restrained King on the throne, with the real power in Parliament. He certainly had no sympathy with the Levellers who wanted Charles dead. On November 11th Cromwell wrote to Walley who was in charge of the King, 'There are rumours about of some intended attempt on his Majesty's person. There-fore I pray you have a care of your guards, for if any such thing should be done, it would be accounted a most horrid act.'[15]

Cromwell was forced to change his mind by the continual scheming of Charles. He wrote, 'It is now expected that the Parliament should govern and defend the kingdom by their own power and not teach the people any longer to expect safety and government from an obstinate man whose heart God had hardened.'[16]

The problem of the King was shelved when the second Civil War broke out in Wales in March 1648 and it was nearly the end of 1648 before Cromwell gained complete victory in what he regarded as an unnecessary and mischievous war. But the end of the Civil War did nothing to end the strife and suspicion in Parliament between the majority Presbyterians and the Independents. Parliament was preparing to replace the King on his throne. The army sent Parliament a demand for the punishment of Charles as 'the grand author of all our troubles'. Cromwell approved of this but Parliament paid no attention so the army employed force. Fairfax captured the King and on December 2nd 1648 occupied London. On December 6th Colonel Pride purged Parliament – forty-five members were arrested and ninety-six excluded. It was now a Parliament of Independents and they turned their attention to deal with the King.

Cromwell still questioned the wisdom of putting Charles on trial if some other way could be found of bringing peace to the nation. But again the question was settled by the King's attitude. He preferred to part with his life rather than with his regal powers, and unless he yielded no constitutional settlement was possible. Cromwell's resistance ended.

Charles was brought to trial on January 20th 1649. The legality of the trial and of the court was greatly disputed. It was objected that the King could not be tried in a court, to which Cromwell answered, 'I tell you we will cut off his head with the crown upon it.' This was typical of Cromwell, having ceased his opposition he was now completely behind the trial. He now came to the conclusion that it was God's will that Charles should die. In many ways it was the second Civil War that swayed Cromwell to this viewpoint. As long as the King lived the peace of England was uncertain and the unnecessary and mischievous war could well be repeated.

The charge of treason was dropped and the King found guilty of being 'public enemy to the commonwealth of England'. He was beheaded ten days later on January 30th 1649. John Owen called the men who brought about the King's death, 'the Lord's workmen' and described the event as 'It is the Lord's doing and is marvellous in our eyes.'[17] There is little doubt that this was a minority view in England. The execution made Charles the tyrant into a martyr and Cromwell into the tyrant.

Ireland

The King's execution swelled the Royalist ranks. In Ireland the Ulster Presbyterians openly declared for Charles 2nd and threw off obedience to Parliament. The question of Ireland was not then whether or not it should be separated from England, for it was certain that Ireland in Royalist hands would be used as a base for an attack on England. So on March 19th 1649 the Council of State nominated Cromwell to command in Ireland. He took his time in preparing his army thoroughly and it was August 13th before Cromwell arrived in Dublin. He was to be in Ireland for nine and a half months and gained victory after victory with very little setback. Generally his treatment of the Irish was one of mercy and generosity. Antonia Fraser says, 'he kept his own soldiers under extremely tight discipline, and two men who were caught plundering hens from some Irish women on the road from Dublin were hanged. In the meantime the country people, being well paid, were content to flock to the parliamentary army and sell it food.'[18] Fraser shows clearly that most of the stories of Cromwell in Ireland could have no possible foundation in fact. Nonetheless the massacres at Drogheda and Wexford were very real

At Drogheda on September 10th nearly 3,000 were put to the sword and at Wexford on October 10th 1,500 were killed. At both places every priest who fell into English hands was put to death. Cromwell offered Drogheda fair and safe terms of surrender but they were refused and a siege followed. Wexford was different and it is certain that Cromwell never intended to destroy the town. On the contrary he wanted it intact to use as winter quarters for his army, but when the soldiers took things into their own hands and ran amok, Cromwell and his officers did nothing to stop them. Charles Firth says, 'when towns were taken by storm, the laws of war authorised the refusal of quarter to their defenders, and on this ground Cromwell justified his action at Drogheda and Wexford. He justified it both on military and political grounds. He had come to Ireland not merely as a conqueror, but as a judge "to ask an account of the innocent blood that had been shed" in the rebellion of 1641, and "to punish the most barbarous massacre that ever the sun beheld,"'[19] He saw himself as the instrument of divine justice, but nothing could change the reality and terribleness of what had happened.

Cromwell was offered the crown of England in 1657 but he rejected it. Instead he remained Lord Protector, a position he received on June 26th 1653 and held this until his death on September 3rd 1658.

Oliver Cromwell has certainly been one of the most controversial characters of English history. Some of the criticism he deserved but it has to be said that he was a man who strongly opposed religious persecution. He was no tyrant and no hypocrite. He was a genuine Christian but far too prone to justify events as the providence of God. He could be warm and sympathetic but at other times harsh and unreasonable.

C. H. Firth sums up Cromwell's life – 'The ideas which inspired his policy exerted a lasting influence on the development of the English state. Thirty years after his death the religious liberty for which he fought was established by law. The union with Scotland and Ireland, which the statesmen of the Restoration undid, the statesmen of the 18th century effected. The mastery of the seas he had desired to gain, and the Greater Britain he had sought to build up became sober realities. Thus others perfected the work which he had designed and attempted... No English ruler did more to shape the future of the land he governed.'[20]

References

1. Antonia Fraser. *Cromwell, our Chief of Men.* Panther 1976. p.7.
2. *Ibid.,* p.17.
3. *Ibid.,* p.35.
4. Charles Firth, *Cromwell.* Putman. 935. p.39.
5. *Ibid.,* p.39.
6. Antonia Fraser, p.666.
7. *Ibid.,* p.67.
8. *Ibid.,* p.68.
9. *Ibid.,* p.74.
10. *Ibid.,* p.86.
11. *Ibid.,* p.97.
12. *Ibid.,* p.100.
13. *Ibid.,* p.101.
14. *Ibid.,* p.148.
15. Charles Firth. *Cromwell.* Oxford University Press. 1958. p.123.
16. Antonia Fraser, p.221.
17. Charles Firth, Putman p.189.
18. Antonia Fraser, p.334.
19. Charles Firth, Putman p.260.
20. *Ibid.,* Putman p.486.

Daniel Rowland (1713 - 1790)

Chapter 6
Daniel Rowland

Daniel Rowland, little known outside his native Wales, is described by J. C. Ryle as 'one of the spiritual giants of the 18th century'. Ryle also said of Rowland, 'Never, perhaps, did any preacher exalt Christ more than Rowland did, and never did any preacher leave behind him such deep and abiding marks in the isolated corner of the world where he laboured.'[1]

Whereas most of the great 18th century preachers had an itinerant ministry, Rowland spent his entire fifty years ministry in a small corner of West Wales. His preaching was so powerful that for all these years huge crowds came to hear him. In an age of great preachers Rowland was second to none. Comparing him to Whitefield a man who heard them both said, 'Whitefield was greater perhaps in the power of alarming the unconverted, but Rowland excelled in building up, strengthening, and comforting the Christian. His sermons were more methodical, and contained more matter and more point. Whitefield's sermons would be soon forgotten; but those of Rowland would be remembered and retained through life.'[2]

Daniel Rowland was born in 1713 near Llangeitho in West Wales. It was a time of spiritual deadness. In 1721 Erasmus Saunders wrote a book entitled *A View of the State of Religion in the Diocese of St. David's*, in which he said, 'So many of our churches are in actual ruins; so many more are ready to fall.'[3] He spoke of men in the ministry who were barely literate and were only there because they were not likely to succeed in any other profession. Although it wasn't a very encouraging picture yet not far from St. David's in West Wales two young boys were growing up who God would use to change the whole spiritual climate of the land. Daniel Rowland was then aged eight years old and Howell Harris was seven. Within thirty years their preaching would change the nation.

Harris was converted when he was twenty years of age. He said of Wales of his day, 'There was at that time a general slumber over the land – neither had anyone whom I knew, the true knowledge of that God whom we pretended to worship – a universal deluge of swearing, lying, reviling, drunkenness, fighting and gaming, had overspread the country like a mighty torrent. Seeing thus rich and poor going as it were hand in hand in the broad way to ruin, my soul was stirred up within me.'[4]

Conversion

Rowland was ordained to the Church of England ministry in 1733 and became curate to his brother at Llangeitho. He was like most of his fellow ministers – unconverted and ungodly. He was converted about 1735 through the preaching of Griffith Jones, one of the few great preachers of that time. Eifion Evans says of him, 'Jones preached feelingly, often with tears running down his cheeks, terrifying the ungodly with the evil and danger of sin, persuading his hearers to flee to Christ for salvation.'[5]

Griffith Jones was preaching near Llangeitho and the curate of the parish went to hear him, not it seems with any spiritual interest but rather with some hostility. At that meeting 'He (Jones) saw a young man in the crowd who appeared restless and rebellious. He observed him for a moment, pointed at him, and with an expression of gentle compassion, exclaimed, "Oh

for a word to reach your heart, young man!" Soon it was
evident that his restlessness had ceased, and he listened earn-
estly for the rest of the sermon; and who was this, but Daniel
Rowland, the curate of the parish. That was the place, and the
way this great man was convicted; great before, in his hostility
to Christ's Gospel and Kingdom, great after that in godliness,
and one of the most eminent ministers that Wales ever saw.'[6]

Immediately Rowland began to preach with a new urgency
and enthusiasm but unfortunately his preaching was limited to
law, judgement and hell. Ryle says, 'At this time, however
curious it may seem, it is clear that Rowland did not preach the
full gospel. His testimony was unmistakably truth, but still it was
not the whole truth. He painted the spirituality and condemning
power of the law in such vivid colours that his hearers trembled
before him, and cried out for mercy. But he did not yet lift up
Christ crucified in all his fullness, as a refuge, a physician, a
redeemer, and a friend; and hence, though many were
wounded, they were not healed.'[7]

A friend spoke to Rowland of this lack in his preaching. He
told him, 'Preach the gospel to the people, dear sir, and apply
the Balm of Gilead, the blood of Christ, to their spiritual wounds,
and show the necessity of faith in the crucified Saviour... If you
go on preaching the law in this manner, you will kill half the
people in the country, for you thunder out the curses of the law,
and preach in such a terrific manner, that no-one can stand
before you.'[8]

The advice was heeded and a new power came into
Rowland's preaching. Thousands were saved and on a
communion Sunday up to 2,000 people would walk many miles
to hear this servant of God. This was no short-term curiosity
but happened continually for nearly fifty years.

The Preacher

Rowland's preaching now knew an unction and authority that can only be explained in terms of the Holy Spirit coming upon him. Soon the church at Llangeitho was too small to contain the crowds who came to hear preaching that was clear, biblical, powerful and challenging.

Preaching is not lecturing, it is heralding forth the word of God. If a preacher's sermons are to touch the hearts of the people, they must first touch the heart of the preacher and Rowland knew his own heart being dealt with by God as he ministered to others. Edward Morgan tells us of the following incident, 'While he was engaged one Sunday morning in reading the church service, his mind was more than usually occupied with the prayers. An overwhelming force came upon his soul as he was praying in those most melting and evangelical words, – "By thine agony and bloody sweat, by thy cross and passion, by thy precious death and burial, by thy glorious resurrection and ascension, and by the coming of the Holy Ghost." This passage is more emphatic in the Welsh language, by reason of an adjective going before the word *agony*, signifying *extreme*. The words, if translated would run thus, – *"by thine extreme agony."* As he uttered these words, a sudden amazing power seized his whole frame; and no sooner did it seize on him, than it ran instantly, like an electrifying shock, through all the people in the church, so that many of them fell down on the ground they had been standing on in a large mass together, there being no pews in the church.'[9]

During week days Rowland began to move outside Llangeitho to preach and it was on one of these visits that he first met Howel Harris, 'In 1737 I came to hear him in Defynnog church in the upper part of our county, where, on hearing the uncommon gifts given him and the amazing power and authority by which he spoke and the effects it had on the people, I was made indeed thankful, and my heart burst with love to God and to him. Here began my acquaintance with him and to all eternity it shall never end.'[10]

Not everyone had such a warm spirit towards Rowland and within the Church of England there was a growing unease with him. Ryle says, 'Rowland, it must be remembered, was never an incumbent. From the time of his ordination in 1733, he was simply curate at Llangeitho, under his elder brother John, until the time of his death in1760... Upon the death of John Rowland, the Bishop of St. David's, who was patron of Llangeitho, was asked to give the living to his brother Daniel, upon the very reasonable ground that he had been serving the parish as curate no less than twenty seven years! The Bishop unhappily refused to comply with this request, alleging as his excuse that he had received many complaints about his irregularities. He took the very singular step of giving the living to John, the son of Daniel Rowland, a young man twenty seven years of age. The result of this very odd proceeding was, that Daniel Rowland became curate to his own son, as he had been curate to his own brother.'[11] In 1763 the Bishop revoked Daniel Rowland's licence to preach and he was ejected from his pulpit at Llangeitho. His friends soon built him a large chapel in Llangeitho and he preached there for the rest of his life.

Revival

God used Rowland and Harris, along with William Williams, in a great work of revival in Wales. Williams said, 'Ignorance, covered the face of Wales, hardly any gospel privilege could stand against the corruption of the day, until about 1738 light broke forth as the dawn in many parts of the world ... and O wonderful day! The Sun shone on Wales. God raised these instruments from the dust and set us with the princes of his people. The net was cast into the sea, and all kinds of fish were caught, great and small. The six southerly counties soon embraced the Word... And this lasted for some years.'[12]

The work of God in Wales has to be seen in the context of what God was doing in America through Jonathan Edwards and in England through Whitefield and the Wesley brothers. The Welshmen were particularly influenced by the writings of Edwards. Eifion Evans says, 'Reading the *Narrative,* the Welsh leaders would have immediately identified with Edwards situation and experiences...they had witnessed effects similar to those spoken of by Edwards... Such was the similarity in the character of the work that Edwards' description of the one (in America) would have served equally well for the other (in Wales).'[13]

Rowland wrote to Whitefield on February 2nd 1743. 'There is a general, fresh, and uncommon stirring in most places. Many come anew under convictions, especially old, worldly professors, and backsliders return. And there is such power as I never felt before given me in preaching and administering of the Lord's Supper.'[14]

Welsh Methodism

With so many converts it was right that Rowland and his fellow preachers should be concerned for their spiritual life and growth. There was little help for a new convert in the churches so fellowship or society meetings were established. Some saw these as divisive but in the circumstances something had to be done to help the new converts. Eifion Evans tells us that, 'Whitefield soon recognised the indispensability of societies to the progress of the revival. As early as 1739 he wrote a letter "to the religious societies lately set on foot in several parts of England and Wales" with the purpose of guiding their meetings. Their purpose was unashamedly experimental, while their teaching function provided a safeguard against morbid introspection and unhealthy exhibitionism.'[15]

These societies were the beginning of Methodism in Wales – always Calvinistic in its doctrine, more in line with Whitefield than Wesley. Eifion Evans says, 'The Calvinism of the Welsh Methodists was not a sterile disputation about words. It produced hearty evangelistic endeavour, vigorous striving for conformity to God's law, and intense personal devotion to the Saviour.' Evans goes on to say, 'The Welsh Methodism of 1740 was kept identifiably one, and doctrinally Calvinistic, by the lively zeal and clear teaching of its leaders. In its essence and character it was simply New Testament Christianity.'[16]

In 1743 at Watford in South Wales, an organisation was formed which became known as 'The Calvinistic Methodist Association.' This took place eighteen months before Wesley held his first Methodist Conference.

Problems

The revival continued for several years but in 1744 serious problems made themselves known. In the 'Association meetings' personal and doctrinal differences between Rowland and Harris became open. If both men had shown more grace the problems could have been avoided but inevitably some believers supported Rowland and some Harris. It was a difficult time for the gospel in Wales but thankfully the work of revival continued and the Holy Spirit's power was still seen. This showed clearly that God is not dependent upon men. Harris withdrew to gather around himself a community at Trefeca in Breconshire. He was not the man he had been. Dallimore makes the point, 'For eleven years Harris had been his (Whitefield) greatest friend. They had been entirely agreed in matters of doctrine, their hearts had been bound together in fellowship and their lives had been united in evangelistic activity. But now Whitefield was confronted with this change – this unseemly and unaccountable behaviour in Harris and therefore with his severing of their joint labour.'[17] This separation of brethren who had been one in the work of the gospel continued until 1762 when thankfully Harris joined again with Rowland and Whitefield.

J. C. Ryle concludes his essay on the life of Daniel Rowland with these words, 'I will wind up this account of Rowland by mentioning a little incident which the famous Rowland Hill often spoke of in his latter days. He was attending a meeting of Methodists Ministers in Wales in one of his visits, when a man, nearly a 100 years old, got up from a corner of the room and addressed the meeting in the following words; – "Brethren, let me tell you this, I have heard Daniel Rowland preach, and I heard him once say, Except your consciences be cleansed by the blood of Christ, you must all perish in the eternal fires." Rowland, at that time, had been dead more than a quarter of a century. Yet, even at that interval, "though dead he spoke". It is a faithful saying, and worthy of all remembrance, that the ministry which exalts Christ crucified most, is the ministry which produces most lasting effects. Never, perhaps, did any preacher exalt Christ more than Rowland did, and never did a preacher leave behind him such deep and abiding marks in the isolated corner of the world where he laboured.'[18]

References

1. Eifion Evans *Daniel Rowland.* BOT 1985 p.1.
2. *Ibid.,* p.4
3. Erasmus Saunders *Welsh Life in the 18th Century,* Country Life 1939. p.118.
4. *Ibid.,* p.138.
5. Eifion Evans p.32.
6. *Ibid.,* p.33.
7. J.C.Ryle *Five Christian Leaders.* BOT, 1960 p.90.
8. Eifion Evans p.43.
9. *Ibid.,* p.50.
10. *Ibid.,* 55 p.52.
11. J.C.Ryle p.95.
12. Eifion Evans p.73.
13. *Ibid.,* p.71.
14. *Ibid.,* p.74.
15. Eifion Evans *Profitable for Doctrine and Reproof.* P&R Studies Conference p.35.
16. *Ibid.,* p.134 &136.
17. Arnold Dallimore *George Whitefield Vol. 2.* BOT, 1980. p. 301.
18. J.C.Ryle p.115.

Jonathan Edwards (1703-58)

Chapter 7

Jonathan Edwards

Jonathan Edwards was born at East Windsor, Connecticut on October 5th 1703. His father Timothy was pastor of the congregational church there for sixty four years. His mother Esther was the daughter of Solomon Stoddard who pastored the church at Northampton, Massachusetts for over 50 years. With such a pedigree it could be assumed that Jonathan would inevitably not only become a Christian but also a preacher. Such an assumption reveals an ignorance of the ways of God. It is divine grace not family privilege that makes a Christian and no one inherits the right to preach. Only God appoints preachers by calling them to serve him.

Nevertheless Jonathan's background was a great privilege and when he was seven or eight years old he was affected by an awakening in his father's church. He wasn't saved at that point but towards the end of his college training he said, 'I was brought to seek salvation in a manner that I never was before. I felt a spirit to part with all things in the world for an interest in Christ. My concern continued and prevailed, with many exercising thoughts and inward struggles; but yet it never seemed to be proper to express that concern by the name of terror.'[1] He was converted some time between March and June in 1721 and wrote about that time, 'I began to have a new kind of apprehension and idea of Christ, and the work of redemption, and the glorious way of salvation by him. An inward, sweet sense of these things, at times, came into my heart; and my soul was led away in pleasant views and contemplation's of them. And my mind was greatly engaged to spend my time in reading and meditating on Christ, on the beauty and excellency of his person, and the lovely way of salvation by free grace in him.'[2]

He was licensed to preach in the summer of 1722. After further years of study, in 1726 he was invited to become assistant to his grandfather Solomon Stoddard at the congregational church at Northampton. Edwards accepted the call and was ordained to the ministry on February 15th 1727 at the age of 24. The same year he married Sarah Pierrepont. So began the ministry of the man who is generally acknowledged to have been the greatest theologian the American churches have produced.

Solomon Stoddard

Stoddard ministered in the town of Northampton, a small Massachusetts community of about 500 people, although this had doubled by the time Jonathan Edwards went there to assist his grandfather. Stoddard was called to pastor the congregational church in 1669 and preached there for two years before he actually accepted the call. The reason for this is not clear except that it may have been that he had a problem with personal assurance of faith. When this was resolved he was ordained in September 1672.

In 1726, at the age of eighty three, although he was still exercising a vigorous ministry and was much loved by his people, it became clear to some that their pastor needed someone to assist him. God had blessed the ministry of Stoddard with many conversions and Christianity in the town was more than a Sunday observance. However there were relatively few men and women who came regularly to the Lord's table. This bothered Stoddard and his answer to the problem was to allow people at the table provided they had a knowledge of Christianity and lived reasonably respectable lives. The sacrament was viewed as a converting ordinance and it was not required for them to have a personal faith in Christ. This was the accepted practice in Northampton and was the situation when Edwards went there in 1727. As a young man of 23 years of age Edwards, who had a great respect for his grandfather, accepted this situation but in later years it was to cause him a great deal of trouble. When Solomon Stoddard died in February 1729, Edwards became pastor of the church.

The Young Pastor

Edwards was a man of great natural ability and an intellect way above most others, but he was also very conscious of his sin. He wrote, 'Often, since I lived in this town, I have had very affecting views of my own sinfulness and vileness; very frequently to such a degree as to hold me in a kind of loud weeping, sometimes for a considerable time together; so that I have often been forced to shut myself up. I have had a vastly greater sense of my own wickedness, and the badness of my heart, than ever I had before my conversion. It is often appeared to me that if God should mark iniquity against me I should appear the very worst of all mankind – of all that have been since the beginning of the world to this time, and that I should have by far the lowest place in hell.'[3]

Such thoughts can either drive a man to despair or throw him more than ever upon the grace of God. Iain Murray says of Edwards, 'He learned by experience, as others had done before him, that while those who have little awareness of the real nature of sin may assert man's ability to repent and believe, to hate sin and love God, those who know the true

condition of human nature can find comfort only in the knowledge that God saves by his sovereign good pleasure and for
the praise of the glory of his grace. Spiritual experience and
sound theology go together.'[4]

It would be very difficult to find any of the great men who
have been used by God who did not share Edwards' view of
themselves. It is not morbid introspection but a spirit sensitive
to the reality of sin's devastating influences. Neither does it render
helpless a preacher who knows the sinfulness of his own heart
but rather it gives urgency to his preaching and a confidence
that the grace of God can save who he wills.

In 1731, at the age of 28, he was invited to preach the
Public Lecture in Boston. He preached on 1 Corinthians 1: 29-31
and spoke powerfully on man's total dependence upon God
for faith and salvation. This set out what was to be the basis of
his ministry throughout his whole life. He said in that sermon,
'Hath any man hope that he is converted, and sanctified, and
that his mind is endowed with true excellency and spiritual
beauty? That his sins are forgiven, and he be received into
God's favour, and exalted to the honour and blessedness of
being his child, and an heir of eternal life? Let him give God all
the glory who alone makes him to differ from the worst of men
in this world, or the most miserable of the damned in hell.'[5]

Revival Preaching

During the years of 1734 and 1735 Northampton experienced
revival. This was to be followed in 1739 by the Great Awakening
which was felt over a far greater area than just Northampton.
Revival is unquestioningly the sovereign work of God and
Jonathan Edwards would have been in total agreement with
the words of Charles Spurgeon – 'No one can revive God's
work, but God himself.' But this does not mean Christians have
nothing to do except to wait for God to move.

In his excellent biography of Edwards, Iain Murray has a powerful chapter entitled, 'The Breaking of the Spirit of Slumber.' He writes, 'It has sometimes been assumed that the preaching of the 18th century leaders in the revivals in North America was simply continuing a well-established tradition. That, however, is not the case. The commonly accepted preaching was not calculated to break through the prevailing formalism and indifference, and the preaching which did bring men to a sense of need and humiliation before God was of a very different order.'[6]

The reason the church needs reviving is that it has lost its way. Spiritual coldness is the product of a lost awareness of the presence of God. One of the main contributors to this is preaching, which though it may still be orthodox, has no power or fire. Edwards wrote of the preaching prior to the Great Awakening, 'I know it has long been fashionable to despise a very earnest and pathetical way of preaching, and they only have been valued as preachers who have shown the greatest extent of learning, strength of reason, and correctness of method and language... An increase in speculative knowledge in divinity is not what is so much needed by our people as something else. Men may abound in this sort of light, and have no heat. How much has there been of this sort of knowledge, in the Christian world, in this age! Was there ever an age wherein strength and penetration of reason, extent of learning, exactness of distinction, correctness of style, and clearness of expression, did so abound? And yet, was there ever an age, wherein there has been so little sense of the evil of sin, so little love to God, heavenly mindedness, and holiness of life, among the professors of the true religion? Our people do not so much need to have their heads stored as to have their hearts touched, and they stand in the greatest need of that sort of preaching which has the greatest tendency to do this.'[7]

Jonathan Edwards believed that sinners cannot be saved unless they first know that they are sinners – 'They do not realise that God sees them when they commit sin and will call them to an account for it. They are stupidly senseless to the importance of eternal things.'[8] Therefore said Edwards, 'Men have to be so dealt with that their conscience stares them in the face and they begin to see their need of a priest and sacrifice.'[9] Murray says, 'Possibly the greatest practical lesson from the 1735 revival for the pulpit of our day is that when ministers have to deal with indifference and unconcern they will simply beat the air unless they begin where the Holy Spirit begins.'[10]

Iain Murray concludes that remarkable chapter, 'The preaching through which the spirit of slumber was broken in the 1730's was searching and convincing. A band of men was being raised up for whom the gravity of sin, the possibility of an unsound profession of Christ, and the carelessness of a lost world were pressing burdens. Behind their public utterances was their vision of God and eternity. Their valleys of personal humiliation had been valleys of vision and, in the words of one who followed in Edwards' steps a century later, "When ministers get a sight of the valley of vision, and of the bottomless gulf into which bone after bone is sinking, they do feel that it is of importance that they should warn and alarm sinners; and then alone do they preach for death, preach for eternity, preach for the judgement seat, preach for heaven and preach, too, for hell."'[11]

Jonathan Edwards was a man who knew his God and had rich experiences of meeting with the Lord. In 1737, whilst alone in the woods, he had a remarkable meeting with his Saviour. He said. – 'The person of Christ appeared ineffably excellent, with an excellency great enough to swallow up all thought and conception – which continued, as near as I can judge, about an hour; which kept me the greater part of the time in a flood of tears, and weeping aloud.' The result of this was a desire 'to lie in the dust, and to be full of Christ alone; to love him with a holy and pure love; to trust in him; to live upon him; to serve and follow him; and to be perfectly sanctified and made pure, with a divine and heavenly purity.' This experience was not an isolated one – 'I have several other times had views very much of the same nature, and which have had the same effects.'[12]

Preachers who meet with God like this will know a true unction when they get into the pulpit and souls will be saved. In the revival of 1734-35, during one period about thirty men and women were converted each week. Edwards says of this time, 'I hope that more than 300 souls were savingly brought home to Christ in this town in the space of half a year, and about the same number of males as females.'[13]

The Great Awakening

After the 1734 revival in Northampton spiritual matters seemed to have declined in people's thinking; but Edwards records that, 'In the year of 1740, in the spring before Mr. Whitefield came to this town, there was a visible alteration; there was more seriousness and religious conversation, especially among young people; ... And thus it continued, until Mr. Whitefield came to town, which was about the middle of October following.'[14]

Whitefield's preaching, on the Sunday of his visit to Edwards, was attended with unusual blessing. He wrote, 'Preached this morning and good Mr. Edwards wept during the whole time of exercise. The people were equally affected; and, in the afternoon, the power increased yet more. I have not seen four such gracious meetings together since my arrival.'[15] When the English man left Northampton the revival did not go with him but increased in power and effect. God uses men in an unusual way in revival but the blessing is not dependent upon them.

The revival at first dealt with many who had already made a profession of faith and these were stirred to greater love for

Christ. The largest number of converts came from those under the age of twenty six years. A new generation was being won for Christ. The revival spread throughout New England and Edwards was called to help and preach in many churches.

On July 8th 1741 he preached at Enfield, Connecticut, an area so far untouched by the revival. He preached a sermon he had previously used in his own church entitled, 'Sinners in the Hands of an Angry God.' Souls were dealt with and were brought to conviction, then repentance and faith, and salvation. This was not unusual and later that year it is recorded at Wethersfield, 'The whole town seems to be shaken... Last Monday night the Lord bowed the heavens and came down upon a large assembly in one of the parishes of the town, the whole assembly seemed alive with distress, the groans and outcries of the wounded were such that my voice could not be heard.'[16]

It is easy to dismiss this sort of preaching as hell fire scraremongering but that is to ignore the supernatural. Men and women were being confronted with their sin and the reality of God's wrath and judgement upon that sin. The power of the preaching could not be explained only in terms of the ability of the preacher. In revival another dimension is added and that is the awesome reality of the presence of God. A young man said of Edwards' preaching that he fully supposed that as soon as the preacher finished his sermon, the Judge would descend and the final separation would take place. Clearly, Jonathan Edwards did not preach 'nice' sermons designed to make his hearers feel comfortable. He confronted men and women with God and the hearers response was not to Edwards but to the God they had offended with their sin. Christianity moved from being a respectable hobby on Sundays to an every day matter of priority and urgency.

There were excesses in the Great Awakening because as Edwards said, 'where God is at work so too will the devil be active.' There was also criticism from some church leaders and Edwards sought to answer these in his writings. He wrote in *Some Thoughts concerning the Present Revival,* – 'If we look back into the history of the church in past ages, we may observe that it has been a common device of the devil to overset a revival of religion; when he finds he can keep men quiet and secure no longer, then he drives them to excesses and extravagances ... that masterpiece of all the devil's works, was to improve the indiscreet zeal of Christians, to drive them into those three extremes of enthusiasm, superstition, and severity towards opposites; which would be enough for an everlasting warning to the Christian church.'[17]

Problems

In 1744 Jonathan Edwards had to face serious problems in his church which led ultimately to his dismissal from the pastorate. He was involved in a matter of discipline among the young people in the church. Edwards had been told that some of those in their early twenties had got hold of a handbook for midwives and this had given rise to obscene talk among them. These youngsters belonged to families in the church and the parents defended their children rather than support what the pastor was trying to do.

Edwards did not handle the difficulty well because when he read a rather long list of young people's names to the church he did not distinguish between those he suspected of being guilty and others. He therefore alienated many families and Dwight said, 'This was the occasion of weakening Mr. Edwards's hands in the work of the ministry, especially among the young people, with whom, by this means, he greatly lost his influence. It seemed in a great measure to put an end to his usefulness at Northampton... He certainly had no visible success after this; the influences of the Holy Spirit were chiefly withheld and stupidity and worldly-mindedness were greatly increased among them.'[18]

Of more serious doctrinal consequence was the basis on which the church at Northampton accepted people into communicant membership. Up until 1740 Edwards had followed the pattern established by his grandfather Solomon Stoddard. A personal profession of faith in Christ was not required, merely a general acceptance of the Christian faith. However, over a period of time Edwards became unhappy with this and felt it contributed to people deceiving themselves as to their true spiritual condition. By 1744 he decided that he could no longer receive someone into membership who did not have a credible profession of personal faith in Christ. He wrote, 'I came to this determination, that if any person should offer to come into the church without a profession of godliness, I must decline being active in his admission.'[19]

A bitter controversy arose and in 1750 he was dismissed from the pastorate by a vote of 230 to 23. Edwards was shocked by this and he wrote, 'I am now separated from the people between whom and me there was once the greatest union. Remarkable is the providence of God in this matter. In this event we have a striking instance of the instability and uncertainty of all things here below.'[20]

The problem had arisen from Stoddard's original error and Dwight said, 'The lax mode of admitting members into the church had prevailed about forty five years, and though both Mr. Stoddard and Mr. Edwards had been most desirous of the prevalence of vital religion in the church, yet, a wide door having been thrown open for the admission of unconverted members, as such, it cannot but have been the fact, that, during this long period, many unconverted members should, through that door, have actually obtained admission into the church... The consequences of Mr. Stoddard's error fell with all their weight on his own grandson.'[21]

It is incredible that a man like Jonathan Edwards, who had known so much revival blessing on his ministry, could be dismissed by such an overwhelming vote. Iain Murray says, 'There is little doubt that the existing prejudices of tradition, backed by the misrepresentations stirred up by leaders in the church and some whom Edwards calls "crafty designing men", account for the sad way in which many Christians acted.'[22]

Stockbridge

Six months after his dismissal Edwards received an invitation from the church in Stockbridge to be their pastor. His work was to be primarily in the mission to Indians and he began his ministry there in August 1751.

The church at Stockbridge was not a happy fellowship and it was not an easy time for Edwards. But Dr. Lloyd-Jones says, 'I believe that in the providence of God he was sent there; because he wrote some of his greatest masterpieces while he was there. In the same way as the imprisonment of John Bunyan for twelve years in Bedford gave us his classics, so, I believe, this isolation of Jonathan Edwards was the means of giving us some of his classics.'[23] In 1757 he was elected to be president of Princeton College but was not there very long and he died on March 22nd 1758.

Jonathan Edwards' contribution to biblical Christianity in the church was and is immense. His books have had a great influence on a new generation of preachers over the last sixty years. Dr. Lloyd-Jones evaluated Edwards in these words, 'Indeed I am tempted, perhaps foolishly, to compare the Puritans to the Alps, Luther and Calvin to the Himalayas, and Jonathan Edwards to Mount Everest! He has always seemed to me to be the man most like the apostle Paul. Of course, Whitefield was a great and mighty preacher as was Daniel

Rowland, but so was Edwards. Neither of them had the mind, neither of them had the intellect, neither of them had the grasp of theology that Edwards had; neither of them was the philosopher he was. He stands out, it seems to me, quite on his own amongst men.'[24]

References

1. Jonathan Edwards, *David Brainerd,* Baker 1992, p.13.
2. Iain Murray *Jonathan Edwards* BOT 1987, p.35.
3. *Ibid.,* p.101.
4. *Ibid.,* p.102-3.
5. *Ibid.,* p.107.
6. *Ibid.,* p.125.
7. *Ibid.,* p.126-7.
8. *Ibid.,* p.128.
9. *Ibid.,* p.129.
10. *Ibid.,* p.130.
11. *Ibid.,* p.133.
12. Lloyd-Jones *The Puritans* BOT 1987 p.357.
13. Iain Murray p.117.
14. *Ibid.,* p.161.
15. *Ibid.,* p.162.
16. *Ibid.,* p.169.
17. *Ibid.,* p.235.
18. *Ibid.,* p.277.
19. *Ibid.,* p.275.
20. *Ibid.,* p.333.
21. *Ibid.,* p.338
22. *Ibid.,* p.340.
23. Lloyd-Jones p.349.
24. *Ibid.,* p.355.

George Whitefield (1714-1770)

Chapter 8
Whitefield in America

Preaching in England in his early twenties, George Whitefield made a tremendous impact where ever he went. Luke Tyerman said, 'In 1737 Whitefield's appearance, voice and pulpit eloquence drew around him thousands… in a succession of public services which literally startled the nation. He was a new phenomenon in the Church of England. All eyes were fixed upon him. His popularity in Bristol, London and other places was enormous. His name became a household word.'[1]

The whole of Whitefield's life could have been occupied with preaching in England, with occasional trips into Scotland and Wales, but God had a broader ministry for this young man. In 1737 he made the first of seven trips to America. Today it takes seven hours to fly from London to New York and seven such journeys during a life time is not unusual, but in the 18th century this was not so. The journey across the Atlantic was dangerous and took a few months each way. Clearly Whitefield saw America as a land to which God wanted him to give a great deal of time.

America was then very much the New World. Georgia had been settled for only five years and Savannah had not much more than a hundred houses. Whitefield had preached to great crowds in London and Bristol but his first congregation in America consisted of seventeen adults and twenty five children. However, after five weeks he wrote, 'America is not so horrid a place as it is represented to be... As to my ministerial office, God (such is his goodness) sets his seal on it here as at other places. We have an excellent Christian school and near a hundred constantly attend at evening prayers ... I visit from house to house, catechise, read prayers twice and expound the two lessons every day; read to a houseful of people three times a week; expound the two lessons at five in the morning, read prayers and preach twice, and expound the catechism to servants, etc., at seven in the evening every Sunday.'[2]

Life in Georgia was hard for the settlers and Whitefield tried to help them materially as well as spiritually. His first step towards this end was to start small schools and an orphanage. From Savannah he moved on to Charleston in South Carolina and it was from here he returned to England in 1738. In just over a year he was back in America again.

America was settled by men and women of deep religious convictions. The words of the Rev. Higginson, one of the leaders of a group of Puritans who left England in 1629, revealed the calibre of the early settlers. He said, 'We go to practise the positive part of church reformation and propagate the gospel in America.'[3] By the beginning of the 18th century something of the early spiritual vigour had diminished but during the years 1720 to 1735 God graciously sent several revivals to the American churches. The Great Awakening began in 1726 in the Dutch reformed churches of the Rariton Valley, New Jersey. Soon Presbyterians like William Tennent were touched by this work of God and by 1734 the Great Awakening had swept the town of Northampton, Massachusetts, through the ministry of the Congregational pastor, Jonathan Edwards.

By 1735 the revival fire began to fade. The churches were left with a rich spiritual heritage but also some serious problems. The American believers heard of the great blessing that attended Whitefield's open air preaching in England and Dallimore says, 'Such news awakened in the hearts of many a

Christian in the Colonies an excitement and fostered a hope that God would send this renowned evangelist to America, and they saw in him the means whereby the revival fires might be rekindled and indeed spread throughout the land. Then word came that Whitefield was on his way to the Colonies and finally that he had arrived in Philadelphia and intended to preach wherever the opportunity afforded throughout the Continent. Such was the situation when Whitefield reached the New World – surely an extraordinary preparation for an extraordinary ministry!'[4]

Whitefield arrived in Philadelphia on October 30th 1739 and from there his ministry reached out to the rest of America – although in practice this meant for him a strip of land along the Atlantic coast about fifty miles wide and 1300 miles long. His preaching was received enthusiastically but this changed when he preached against the coldness and formality of much church life. Almost all the Church of England clergy in America were offended by this and opposed Whitefield.

Benjamin Franklin, who was not a Christian, wrote, 'In 1739 there arrived among us the Rev. Mr. Whitefield. He was at first permitted to preach in some of the churches; but the clergy, taking a dislike to him, soon refused him their pulpits and he was obliged to preach in the fields … He had a loud and clear voice, and articulated his words and sentences so perfectly, that he might be heard and understood at a great distance, especially as his audiences, however numerous, observed the most exact silence.'[5] Franklin was intrigued to know how effective Whitefield's voice was in reaching the crowds and did some calculations – 'I computed that he might well be heard by more than 30,000. This reconciled me to the newspaper accounts of his having preached to 25,000 people in the fields.'[6]

In two months Whitefield travelled the land from New York to Savannah and preached to huge crowds. He left Charleston in January 1740 for England. Of his second visit to America he said, 'It is now the 75th day since I arrived at Rhode Island. My body was then weak, but the Lord has much renewed its strength. I have been enabled to preach, I think, a 175 times in public, besides exhorting frequently in private. I have travelled upwards of 800 miles, and gotten upwards of £700, in goods, provisions, and money, for the Georgia orphans. Never did I perform my journeys with so little fatigue, or see such a continuance of the divine presence in the congregations to whom I have preached. Praise the Lord, O my soul.'[7]

Five more visits were made by Whitefield to America and he was used greatly by God in the work of the gospel there although his work was not confined to preaching.

Bethesda

From his first visit to America Whitefield had a particular concern for orphans. To help these children would cost a great deal of money but this did not deter Whitefield. The condition of orphan children in 18th century America seemed to be the concern of very few people and the sort of care given them today was unheard of then. Whitefield was ploughing in an almost new field. The idea for an orphanage had first been put to him by Charles Wesley who had heard of similar homes established in Germany. Whitefield recognised that the need was there in Georgia and he set about doing something about it.

It was not until January 1740 that he was able to go with some friends and view 500 acres of land ten miles from Savannah. It was here that he built the orphanage – 'I called it "Bethesda", that is, "The House of Mercy"; for I hope many acts of mercy will be shown there.' It would be many months before Bethesda was ready but the need was great there so Whitefield rented the largest house in Savannah to immediately accommodate twenty four orphans. Several years later he said of this venture, 'Had I proceeded according to the rules of prudence, I should have first cleared the land, built the house, and then taken in the orphans; but I found their condition so pitiable, and the inhabitants so poor, that I immediately opened an infirmary, hired a large house at a great rent, and took in at different times twenty four orphans.'[8] The problem was that Whitefield forgot he was building in what he called 'by far the most expensive part of all His Majesty's dominions'. This caused him enormous problems in meeting his financial obligations.

Building and maintaining an orphanage was both a huge task and a very expensive one. Collections had to be made in the churches. The first was made in March at Charleston and raised £70. By June, Whitefield had collected over £500. The collections continued wherever he preached because he had undertaken to meet the full financial responsibility for Bethesda. His biggest problem however, came from the Trustees. The difference between Whitefield and these men caused the preacher much heartache. He wrote, 'I am tempted to wish I had never undertaken the Orphan House.'[9]

Some may be tempted to think that Whitefield took on too much and should have confined himself to his preaching. But the pastoral heart that undoubtedly contributed to making him such a great preacher could not ignore the pitiable condition of America's orphans. William Cowper said of Whitefield,

> He followed Paul – his zeal a kindred flame,
> His apostolic charity the same.

Whitefield and the American Preachers

Because his Calvinistic doctrines were not always acceptable, some pulpits were closed to Whitefield in America as they were in Britain. A letter to *The Boston Post Boy* on June 23rd 1740 said, 'Mr. Whitefield and his adherents have infatuated the multitude with the doctrines of regeneration, free grace, conversion, etc., representing them as essential articles of religion, though in reality they are inconsistent with true religion, and are subversive of all order and decency, and repugnant to common sense.'[10] Later that year Whitefield found that the refusal by the Church of England to allow him to preach only served to increase his popularity with the people. Then the Quakers, who did not like his doctrine of original sin, also began to criticise Whitefield. At this point the Dissenters were still sympathetic but Whitefield was already anticipating problems from them. It is never easy to be criticised publicly so he truly valued the support received from men who really believed the Word of God. Whitefield also had great respect for many of the American preachers. Of Gilbert Tennent he said, 'Never before heard I such a searching sermon. He went to the bottom indeed, and did not daub with untempered mortar. He convinced me, more and more, that we can preach the gospel of Christ no further than we have experienced the power of it in our lives. I found what a babe and novice I was in the things of God.'[11]

Jonathan Edwards's wife Sarah wrote to her brother about Whitefield, 'It is wonderful to see what a spell he casts over an audience by proclaiming the simplest truths of the Bible. I have seen upwards of a 1000 people hang on his words with breathless silence, broken only by an occasional half suppressed sob. He impresses the ignorant, and not less the educated and refined. It is reported that while the miners of England listened to him, the tears made white furrows down their smutty cheeks. So here, our mechanics shut up their shops, and the day labourers throw down their tools, to go and hear him preach, and few return unaffected... He speaks from a heart all aglow with love, and pours out a torrent of eloquence which is almost irresistible. Many, very many persons in Northampton date the beginning of new thoughts, new desires, new purposes, and a new life, from the day on which they heard him preach of Christ and his salvation. Perhaps I ought to tell you that Mr. Edwards and some others think him in error on a few practical points; but his influence on the whole is so good we ought to bear with little mistakes.'[12] This was high praise indeed but Sarah Edwards' concluding words to her brother are interesting.

Clearly Jonathan Edwards and other leaders did not agree with Whitefield on everything but they continued to work with him and welcomed him to their pulpits. In spite of their differences the American preachers recognised the unusual way God was using the English man and praised God for it. Samuel Davies had heard Whitefield preach in London and commented that whilst the sermon was ordinary the unction was extraordinary.

This was very much the spirit of Whitefield himself. There were major doctrinal differences between him and John Wesley but still Whitefield delighted in the way the Lord was using Wesley. It is only men of little vision and little heart who find it necessary to divide over every controversy. Bigger men can cope with such things and do not fail to recognise that God can use others as well as them. This does not mean that they are weak on doctrinal convictions; on the contrary, their doctrine is so strong as not to feel threatened by someone who does not agree 100% with them. So Jonathan Edwards was able to write, 'Mr. Whitefield preached four sermons in the meetinghouse (besides a private lecture at my house). The congregation was extraordinarily melted by each sermon, almost the whole assembly being in tears for a greater part of the time. Mr. Whitefield's sermons were suitable to the circumstances of the town; containing just reproofs of our backslidings, and in a most moving and affectionate manner, making use of our great profession and great mercies, as arguments with us to return to God, from whom we had departed.'[13]

Contributions

Whitefield's influence in America was great particularly when
one considers that he was not American. Clearly he loved the
country and its people and about a third of his whole ministry
of thirty four years was spent either crossing the Atlantic or
preaching in America.

As well as a concern for children Whitefield felt deeply the
plight of slaves brought from Africa to the USA. As he did in all
things he felt it necessary to make this concern known. In 1740
he wrote a letter to the inhabitants of Maryland, Virginia, North
and South Carolina concerning their slaves; 'How you will
receive it I know not; but whatever be the event, I must inform
you in the meekness and gentleness of Christ, that God has a
quarrel with you for your cruelty to the poor Negroes. Whether
it be lawful for Christians to buy slaves, I shall not take it upon
me to determine, but I am sure that it is sinful, when bought, to
use them worse than brutes. And I fear the generality of you,
who own Negroes, are liable to such a charge, for your slaves,
I believe, work as hard as the horses whereon you ride.'[14]

The letter was published by Benjamin Franklin and caused
deep resentment in a nation in which slavery had become a
normal part of life. Whitefield not only wrote about slavery but
also took practical steps to help them by buying 5,000 acres of
land in Philadelphia and building a large house. As well as this
he was one of the first to preach to the slaves. Dallimore says,
'It is probable that more preachers of that day would have been
willing to carry their message to the Negroes but failed to do so
because of the difficulty inherent in preaching to so primitive a
people. But Whitefield's gifts – his ability to simplify divine truths
and to present the narratives of the Scriptures and the message
of the gospel with vivid clarity – rendered him particularly suited
to such a ministry. In turn, the Negroes found an unusual interest in his preaching, and many of them testified that God used
it in bringing his grace to their hearts.'[15]

Whitefield was never one to court popular favour and his ministry to the Negroes showed this. He also opposed, together with men like William and Gilbert Tennent, the unconverted being ministers and preaching the gospel, a practise which was common in New England. Whitefield was not slow to add his weight to their case. His opposition was vocal, uncompromising, perhaps somewhat rash but not without success. When he returned to America in 1744 he heard of twenty ministers in the Boston area who had been converted as a result of his speaking on this matter. This was not confined to Boston and in many towns pastors told him of their conversion because of his preaching on the evil of an unconverted ministry.

It was inevitable that this emphasis should arouse opposition and pamphlets were written against him. Whitefield clearly felt the pain of ridicule and opposition but he believed it was a price worth paying to expose such a serious problem. Joseph Tracy writes, 'Nor was this all. Many truly pious ministers had a very low standard of duty, of hope and of effort. They were scarce aware that anything was required of them, besides the conscientious performance of a certain round of official services. These being performed, they trusted that God would add his blessing, whether they could see any signs of it or not … Many such pastors were awakened to new views of ministerial duty, learnt to be no longer satisfied without manifest evidence of usefulness, and thence forth laboured to produce ascertainable changes among the people of their charge. On the whole, the beneficial influence of revival on the ministry was immense.'[16]

Clearly Whitefield's greatest contribution was his preaching and thousands were converted under his ministry both in Britain and America. He was an evangelist who preached with divine unction to huge congregations. The significance of such an unusual ministry did not finish with the death of the preacher. In the 19th century Charles Spurgeon said, 'There is no end to

the interest which attaches to such a man as George Whitefield. Often as I have read his life, I am conscious of distinct quicken-
ing whenever I turn to it. He *lived*. Other men only seem to be
half alive; but Whitefield was all life, fire, wing, force. My own
model, if I may have such a thing in due subordination to my
Lord, is George Whitefield; but with unequal footsteps must I
follow in his glorious track.'[17]

References

1. Arnold Dallimore *George Whitefield* Vol 1. BOT 1980, p.446.
2. *Ibid.,* p.202
3. S.M. Houghton *Sketches of Church History* BOT 1980, p.172.
4. Arnold Dallimore, p.429.
5. *Ibid.,* p.439.
6. *Ibid.,* p.439.
7. Partridge *The Moorfield Preacher.* p.5.
8. Partridge *The Moorfield Preacher.* p.37.
9. Arnold Dallimore, p.462.
10. *Ibid.,* p.478.
11. Joseph Tracy *The Great Awakening* BOT 1976, p.53.
12. Iain Murray *Jonathan Edwards* p.162.
13. Arnold Dallimore, p.538.
14. *Ibid.,* p.495.
15. *Ibid.,* p.500
16. Joseph Tracy p.393-4.
17. Arnold Dallimore, p.534.

Charles Finney (1792-1875)

Asahel Nettleton (1783-1844)

Chapter 9
Nettleton and Finney

When George Whitefield visited America for the first time in 1737, Jonathan Edwards had already experienced the blessings of revival. In 1734 and again in 1735 remarkable demonstrations of Holy Spirit power had been seen in New England. Between 1740 and 1742 there was a fresh outbreak of revival preceding and attending Whitefield's visit to Northampton; a period known as the 'Great Awakening'. By 1756 the spiritual climate had changed again and Edwards wrote, 'God indeed is remarkably frowning upon us everywhere, our enemies get above us very high and we are brought down very low ... What will become of us God only knows?'[1] War was in the land; first the French and Indian war and then the Revolutionary War; all of which served to quench the influence of the revival.

Asahel Nettleton

It was at this period, seven years after independence was won, that Asahel Nettleton was born in 1783. He lived for nearly sixty years and his life spanned the Second Great Awakening. This revival was between 1792 and 1808 but its influence was still strong well into the 1830s.

Nettleton's parents were not very religious but under the terms of the 'half way covenant' he was baptised at six days old. This covenant allowed parents who themselves had not made a profession of faith but had been baptised as infants, to bring their children for baptism. The children were then considered to be 'half-way' members but were not allowed to attend the Lord's Table.

He was brought up to learn the Catechism and the Calvinism of his day was embedded in his mind. He was converted when he was eighteen years of age during the revival of 1801 at Killingworth, Connecticut, although for the previous ten months he had been under deep conviction of sin. Thornbury says, 'Peace did not dawn in his soul with dramatic suddenness. Somewhat gradually the nightmare of terror passed away and some stability was restored in a rational domain where "King Reason" was nearly driven from his seat... He had learnt the hard way that salvation is by grace – now he relished this truth... Such a fundamental change in one's view of the Deity, the way of salvation, and ordinary Christian responsibilities, we can safely declare to be marks of regeneration. Asahel had been converted. An unseen hand had snatched him from the yawning gulf of destruction. He was now a child of God and peace filled his heart.'[2]

He was now a saved man and went back to the work on the farm but God had other plans for him. Soon there began to stir in his soul a burden for lost souls. He said, 'If I might be the means of saving one soul, I would prefer it to all the riches and honours of this world.'[3] This is a healthy frame of mind in a young convert. Nettlton's great desire was to be a missionary and to take the gospel to those who had never heard it. He realised he needed an education but this seemed impossible when in 1802 both his father and brother died in an epidemic. He was needed at home now more than ever but his desire was greater than the obstacles. He studied after work under the tuition of his minister and by the autumn of 1805 he was qualified to enter the freshman's class at Yale.

The college was anything but godly although the president was the godly Timothy Dwight, a grandson of Jonathan Edwards. Nettleton was the only Christian in the freshman class so consequently he had few close friends. He was quiet, shy, and modest and something of an introvert but his devout character stood out so that Timothy Dwight was led to say, 'He will make one of the most useful men this country has ever seen.'[4] This was said in spite of the fact that at best Nettleton was only of average ability academically. He plodded through his studies and finished at Yale in 1809.

Theologically he was very much in line with Jonathan Edwards and various doctrinal controversies at Yale had caused him to think through his beliefs. He knew what he believed; he was a Calvinist and was also convinced that revivals and spiritual awakenings were blessings sent down from God. So at the age of twenty eight Nettleton was a shy man, not outstanding in studies but thoroughly grounded in the doctrines of grace. He had a great love for his God and a passion for souls but was uncertain as to which way the Lord was leading him.

Charles Finney

Finney was born nine years after Nettleton in 1792 in Connecticut. When he was two years of age his parents moved to Oneida, in New York State, which at that time was practically a wilderness. They were not Christians and Finney had little or no religious training. He said, 'I seldom heard a sermon, unless it was an occasional one from some travelling minister, or some miserable holding forth of an ignorant preacher who would sometimes be found in that country. I recollect very well that the ignorance of the preachers that I heard was such, that the people would return from meeting and spend a considerable time in irrepressible laughter at the strange mistakes which had been made and the absurdities which had been advanced.'[5]

He knew no Christian influence at all until he was twenty years old, when he moved to the town of Adams to study law. There he began to attend the Presbyterian church and came under the ministry of Rev. George Gale. Finney did not appreciate the preaching and writes, 'His preaching was of the old school type; that is, it was thoroughly Calvinistic; and whenever he came out with the doctrines, which he seldom did, he would preach what has been called hyper-Calvinism. He was, of course, regarded as highly orthodox; but I was not able to gain very much instruction from his preaching. As I sometimes told him, he seemed to me to begin in the middle of his discourse, and to assume many things which to my mind needed to be proved. He seemed to take it for granted that his hearers were theologians, and therefore that he might assume all the great and fundamental doctrines of the gospel. But I must say that I was rather perplexed than edified by his preaching.'[6]

Whether or not Gale was a hyper-Calvinist is open to doubt. Certainly in later years Finney often used the term incorrectly and dubbed all Calvinists as hyper. In spite of Finney's criticism of Gale's preaching, during his first year at Adams sixty five converts were added to the church. It was at this time that Finney bought his first Bible and began also to attend the prayer meeting. But he continued to be critical of both the church and its minister. From Charles Finney's own memoirs we can see it was a praying church, conscious of its need of the outpouring of the Holy Spirit and with the great desire to see souls saved. The ministry was biblical and convicted Finney that he was 'by no means in a state of mind to go to heaven if I should die.'[7] He was three years in the church before he became a Christian in 1821. In this year revival came again to Adams but although over 100 people were converted at this time, which must have had a significant influence upon his spiritual state, it is strange that he always maintained that neither the revival in the town nor the ministry in the church had any bearing on his conversion. None the less his conversion experience had all the marks of a true work of grace.

Immediately he wanted to preach the gospel and soon left the legal profession to study for the ministry. In March 1824 he was licensed to preach by the Presbyterians. He had all the natural attributes for public preaching. Thornbury says, 'Charles Finney was marvellously equipped to be a public speaker. Tall and handsome, he had hawk-like eyes which could nearly hypnotise those upon whom his gaze fell while speaking. He had a mellow, wide-ranging voice and exuded poise and self-assurance. Almost from the beginning of his public ministry, all who heard him were captivated by his stage presence. As one has said he had a dramatic talent that made him one of the best pulpit actors of his day. He put his whole body into his preaching, and in his early days writhed, gesticulated, and groaned so in the pulpit that unfriendly observers thought him coarse, crazy, or hypocritical. Many found him inspiring and instructive.'[8]

His doctrine however, to put it mildly, was far from satisfactory. He ridiculed the truth of the imputation of our sin to Christ, and to quote his own words, 'The sin of all the elect, both original and actual – that is, the guilt of Adam's sin, together with the guilt of their sinful nature, and also guilt of their personal transgressions, are all literally imputed to Christ; and therefore the divine government regarded him as an embodiment of all the sins and guilt of the elect, and treated him accordingly; that is, the Father punished the Son precisely as much as all the elect deserved. Hence their debt being thus fully discharged by the punishment of Christ, they are saved upon the principle of exact justice.'[9] This is a fair summary of what the Bible teaches but Finney regarded it as 'theological fiction', as also he did the doctrine of Christ's righteousness being imputed to us.

Of the Westminster Confession of Faith he said, 'When I came to read the *Confession of Faith*, and saw the passages that were quoted to sustain these peculiar positions, I was absolutely ashamed of it. I could not feel any respect for a document that would undertake to impose on mankind such dogmas as those, sustain, for the most part, by passages of Scripture that were totally irrelevant; and not in a single instant sustained by passages which, in a court of law, would have been considered at all conclusive.'[10] Paul Cook says of this statement by Finney that he 'betrays what is the over ruling criterion of all his thinking in assessing the rightness or wrongness of doctrine; it is the rational principle. Finney would accept nothing in his system of thought which was not immediately intelligible and reasonable to the mind of men...There could be little recognition of divine grace because man never accepts by the light of natural reason his need of total dependence upon God as Lord and Saviour.'[11]

So here is Finney at the age of thirty two years, beginning to preach and very confident in his own ability and reason. He had a strong dominant character, determined to go its own way. The old doctrines so precious to Edwards and Nettleton he dismissed as theological fiction.

Nettleton's Preaching

Nettleton began to preach in an area of Connecticut known as the 'wasted places'; so called because the churches were small in membership, lifeless and unable to support a full time pastor. This was the legacy of the havoc caused by James Davenport sixty years earlier. Davenport moved from parish to parish and without invitation intruded into other men's ministries and churches. He encouraged revolt by members against their pastors and urged them to leave the churches. Ministers who opposed him were labelled 'Pharisees' and 'letter-learned', but spiritually dead. The damage done to the churches, many of which had known revival, was so great that sixty years later it was still very evident.

From this Nettleton learned many lessons on how itinerant preachers ought to conduct themselves. For the rest of his ministry he would not intrude into a parish without the invitation of the local pastor. He regarded any other approach as one which would destroy and not promote the work of the gospel.

In 1813, at the invitation of Lyman Beecher, Nettleton spent three to four months preaching at Milton. The church there was weak and plagued with divisions but they soon recognised that God had sent them a very special man. Thornbury writes, 'The man in their midst was a marked individualist, as seen in a remark he made after one of the evening meetings. He told them that he had come at the request of others and that a revival was his goal and should be theirs. He urged them to pray for a spiritual awakening. "Whether you do or not", he said matter of factly, "it is possible there may be one for Christians in other places have agreed to pray for you." Such talk, reflecting a man totally confident in his God stunned them at first, but he eventually won their hearts.'[12]

At Milton, as Nettleton preached on the holiness of God, the law, hell, and the need of repentance, the Spirit of God brought revival to the town. Nettleton's preaching was anything but superficial and this was reflected in the type of converts seen. To quote Thornbury again, 'to be converted under the ministry of Nettleton was to become Calvinistic in theology. Such ideas as total depravity, the necessity of regeneration, justification through Christ alone, and the sovereignty of God in salvation, were not only believed but felt. Any notion of dependence on the merits of man's free will as a cause or ground of salvation were routed. The doctrines of grace were meat, bread, butter and milk to those who came to salvation under Nettleton's preaching.'[13] His ministry when he visited a church would be firstly to preach at the ordinary services urging the believers to repent of their sin and seek the Lord's blessing. When God began to move in people's hearts and the unsaved began to seek salvation, Nettleton would arrange an inquiry meeting. These were not held in the church but other buildings. The meetings were usually quiet and reverent as he spoke to individuals. This would be followed by an address to everyone, and says Thornbury, 'Inquiry meetings were simply clinics for those in spiritual trouble. Nettleton was the doctor, his scalpel was the law and his medicine was the gospel. Thousands came out of those clinics cured.'[14]

Asahel Nettleton was truly a remarkable servant of God. As a preacher he was good enough to be compared with Whitefield. Although today he is largely forgotten, his influence upon his day was enormous. That such a man, so owned and blessed by God, should be forgotten speaks volumes of the spiritual degeneracy of evangelicalism today.

Finney's Preaching

Finney began to preach in the small towns of Jefferson County going first to Evans' Mill and Antwerp. He said the people there 'extolled my preaching' and 'thronged the place to hear me preach'. In spite of this he could not get the people to respond in the way he wanted so after two or three weeks he resorted to rather dramatic means – 'I then said to them, now I must know your minds, and I want that you who have made up your minds to become Christians, and will give your pledge to make your peace with God immediately, should rise up; but that, on the contrary, those of you who are resolved that you will not become Christians and wish me so to understand, and wish

Christ so to understand, should sit still.'[15] The people were angry with this but a deacon of the church said to Finney. 'Brother Finney, you have got them.' The deacon was right but it does raise the question as whether the resulting so called revival was due to the work of the Holy Spirit or the methods of Charles Finney?

From 1825 to 1832 Finney was involved in what were called the 'Western Revivals'. The problem was that the results of this work were very short lived. James Boyle, who had worked with Finney in these revivals, wrote to him on Christmas day 1834, 'Let us look over the fields where you and others and myself have laboured as revival ministers, and what is now (two years later) their moral state? What was their state within three months after we left them? I have visited and revisited many of these fields, and groaned in spirit to see the sad, frigid, carnal, contentious state into which the churches have fallen – and fallen very soon after our first departure from among them.'[16]

Finney himself said in 1851 that his early converts 'soon relapse again into their former state'. This he attributed to the fact that he had taught an imperfect doctrine of sanctification, but probably nearer to the truth is that he taught an imperfect doctrine of regeneration and justification. If he regarded the *Westminster Confession of Faith* to be theological fiction it is not surprising that his preaching produced converts who were in his own words, 'a disgrace to religion'.

The 'new measures' which Finney used resulted in basic doctrinal deficiency but what was perhaps more disturbing was Finney's attitude towards pastors and their churches. Like Davenport he sought to destroy the pastor's authority and to undermine the respect in which he was held. The result was what Nettleton called 'civil war in Zion'. The reasons for this attitude were again doctrinal. Finney had a great dislike for Calvinists, which in effect meant nearly all the ministers of the day. Thornbury says, 'As Finney went from place to place, building all the while a large following, he considered it essential, in moving into a community or church, to crush whatever strongholds there might be of people who held to inherited depravity and sovereign grace in salvation. Sinners were told everywhere that they needed no special divine agency to convert them, and they reacted by professing faith in thousands. Many pastors and lay men, who had formally held to Calvinism found him too formidable an adversary and yielded to his verbal hammer strokes. Finney soon came to regard himself as a crusader against the status quo; a prosecuting attorney bent on convicting and sentencing systems opposed to his own.'[17]

The 'New Measures' Controversy

'Civil war in Zion' was no exaggeration. The 'new measures' controversy caused a great stir and much bitterness in the churches. In order to try and bring peace Nettleton was urged to meet Finney. By this time Nettleton was a sick and tired man and reluctant for a meeting. But two meetings did take place at the end of 1826. Finney was not a man to be influenced by anyone and Nettleton did not handle the meetings well. The result therefore was that nothing was solved.

Finney says of the meetings, 'I had had the greatest confidence in Mr. Nettleton though I had never seen him. I had had the greatest desire to see him; so much so that I had frequently dreamed of visiting him, and obtaining information from him in regard to the best means of promoting a revival. I felt like sitting at his feet, almost as I would at the feet of an apostle, from what I had heard of his success in promoting revivals. At that time my confidence in him was so great that I think he could have led me, almost or quite, at his discretion.'[18] In spite of this high estimation he said he had for Nettleton, in the next page of his memoirs Finney goes on to say, 'I saw enough to satisfy me that I could expect no advice or instruction from him, and that he was there to take a stand against me.'[19]

In 1831 Finney, in seeking still new methods to strengthen his ministry, turned to the old Methodist camp meeting practice of the 'anxious seat'. Men like Jonathan Edwards or George Whitefield, who had seen thousands converted under their preaching, never used the 'anxious seat' or public invitation. Finney began to make the 'anxious seat' the test of whether or not someone was sincere in seeking Christ. The physical act of coming forward was seen as a sign of submission to God. This was the forerunner of the present day invitation system.

The 'new measures' split the churches and there was no way of resolving such fundamental doctrinal differences. Nettleton died in 1844 and Finney in 1875. Nettleton is by and large forgotten and if it were not for two books published in1975 and 1977, would have been completely forgotten. On the other hand Finney, through his books *Memoirs* and *Lectures on Revival* , has had an enormous effect on evangelicalism right up to the present day.

Finney's doctrine and methods pander to man's natural desires not to be too dependent upon God. Thornbury makes this devastating assessment of Finney, 'he more or less democratised the kingdom of God, making man sovereign and putting God up for vote.'[20] Finney's idea that it was possible to have a revival any time, plus his use of the 'anxious seat', guaranteed results. This was most welcome to churches and his revivalism has become today's evangelicalism. The baffling thing is that 'Finneyism' was born during a period of genuine revival. Nettleton had seen thousands converted under his preaching. Was the real problem the lack of spiritual awareness and doctrinal depth of the Calvinistic ministers of the day? No one, including Nettleton, challenged Finney on his doctrine, only on his methods. But methods are only the inevitable outcome of what a preacher doctrinally believes.

References

1. J.F. Thornbury *God Sent Revival* EP 1977, p.23.
2. *Ibid.*, p.32.
3. *Ibid.*, p.34.
4. *Ibid.*, p.37.
5. Charles Finney *Memoirs* Hodder & Stoughton p.4.
6. *Ibid.*, p.7.
7. *Ibid.*
8. J.F. Thornbury p.159.
9. Charles Finney p.57.
10. *Ibid.*, p.60.
11. Paul Cook *One Steadfast High Intent* pp.6-7.
12. J.F. Thornbury p.60.
13. *Ibid.*, p.65.
14. *Ibid.*, p.115.
15. Charles Finney p.63.
16. Paul Cook p.13.
17. J.F. Thornbury pp.161-2.
18. Charles Finney p.202.
19. *Ibid.*, p.303.
20. J.F. Thornbury p.203.

Finally...

Do great men make the events or do great events make the men? Probably both are true. It certainly requires the right man to get events moving but then the significance of the unfolding drama will draw out from the men the greatness that God had placed in them for such a time.

God never has to look around for the right man at any given time. He has already determined whom he is going to use and completely endowed that man with all the necessary abilities required. Natural characteristics plus special gifts are all used by the Holy Spirit to accomplish what the Lord has determined. Luther's bullishness and enthusiasm were crucial to the Reformation. He did not know how to compromise and this was needed in his dealings with the Roman church. But of course this alone cannot explain the Reformation. Here was the greatest work of God outside of Scripture and it needed a man whose faith and trust was in God, not natural abilities.

The men we have looked at were different in temperament and outlook but they were usable to God because they loved him, loved his word and saw service to the Lord as the highest possible calling. Probably the common factor was their love for the truth of Scripture. They were willing to suffer and die for this.

They were not men seeking greatness. Jonathan Edwards would be amazed to think that his books are still valued in the twenty first century. When Martin Luther nailed his 95 theses to the door of the church at Wittenburg he had no idea what this would lead to. Whitefield hated the thought of fame. He was concerned only for the glory of his Saviour and was willing for the name of Whitefield to perish.

Spiritual men do not look for fame and the applause of people; they are concerned only with being faithful to God. Faithfulness is more valuable in gospel work than greatness. It always honours the Lord and is concerned with his glory not its own. Few will be great but all of us should be faithful. Out of that may flow greatness but if it does not then the Lord is still honoured.

Other titles by Peter Jeffery published by Evangelical Press

Bitesize theology - an ABC of the Christian faith

Enjoying God always - 366 daily readings

How shall they hear? - church-based evangelism

How to behave in church? - a guide to church life

The Lord's supper - important questions that many may ask about this ordinance

Opening up Ephesians - a young people's study of Ephesians

Overcoming life's difficulties - learning from the book of Joshua

Rainbow of grace - learning from the life of Noah

Salvation exposed! - God's way of salvation

Sickness and death in the Christian family - finding rest and encouragement in God in times of stress and loss

Struggling but winning - a survival guide for Christians

What you need to know about salvation - a day-by-day guide to the Christian life

Which way to God? - who is God? what is man? what is sin? who is Jesus Christ?

You can't fool God - biblical characters whose delusions serve as a vital lesson to us all

The young Spurgeon - his childhood, conversion, and first experiences as a preacher

A wide range of excellent books on spiritual subjects is available from Evangelical Press. Please write to us for your free catalogue or contact us by e-mail.

Evangelical Press
Faverdale North Industrial Estate, Darlington, DL3 OPH, England

Evangelical Press USA
PO Box 84, Auburn, MA 01501, USA

e-mail sales: sales@evangelicalpress.org

web: http://www.evangelicalpress.org